# Above & Below This Reality

## The Lost Encrypted Knowledge

# Above & Below This Reality

## The Lost Encrypted Knowledge

Melynda Pearce

# CONTENTS

# INTRODUCTION

## MY REASON TO EXIST

I believe my purpose in this current life has been to seek the truth and reconnect to what was missing within my reality. I have made many important discoveries while on this journey we call "life". In 2000, the most significant event and discoveries of my life occurred. My existence in this consciousness was forever changed...for the better. That day, I clinically died. I flatlined. For three days I lay in a comatose state, somewhere in time and space. While my fragile life barely kept the medical devices beeping, I experienced what I have come to believe was another realm of existence and reality. It was that 3 days, 72 hours, that changed my life forever and led me to find my future, our path. While my body was medically and officially dead, I intrinsically understood that I originated from another dimension of existence, long, long ago.

From the 73rd hour, when I crashed back to my recovery bed, through this minute, I have learned and accepted an entirely new and profound way to see my very existence.

Uppermost of my self-discovery is the realization that I had pledged to undertake a quest ...for The "Anointed One", "Christ". I vividly recall meeting him face-to-face (as if I could ever forget!). He spoke to me about my life and my purpose. He spoke to me, gently, about what I must do, and for how long I must do it, in this life, or the next, or the next. I have a quest and I am going to explain to everyone who will listen.

This information is vital to all our lives. In the coming chapters you will understand Love, Gratitude, Reality, the Christ Consciousness and The Coming Third Peril. You will learn why many are determined to master space exploration of Mars and to also colonize that planet. The true definitions of these and other important concepts are the Encrypted Knowledge in all of us. We have done this before. That knowledge has been dormant, inaccessible, yet waiting to be rediscovered by all of us. Read my words and see the truth. It will change your life.

## REVEALED KNOWLEDGE

- ▲ It is important for each human to understand that they are here for a much grander purpose than to be limited by their reality.
- ▲ All humans must understand that we are participating in a false reality, robbing us of our reason to exist.
- ▲ No one will ever own this planet.
- ▲ Each human has a minimum responsibility to themselves to seek their higher purpose. No one in this consciousness is exempt from this discovery.
- ▲ I have sought out my purpose and discovered it is larger than my multiple lives put together.
- ▲ Understand the Knowledge deeply buried under multiple layers of man's false realities. Raise your consciousness while you are alive now.
- ▲ I exist in one reality, with elements of numerous experiences. To master the ability to separate the false from the real is astounding to say the least.

## CHRIST CONSCIOUSNESS: THE LOST KNOWLEDGE

Be the archaeologist of your mind - together we can dig for the truth buried within!

We will journey together to rediscover the mystery of the lost Knowledge. We will trace how all Religions created the path for it to be buried until now.

Although we had previously been aware of this Knowledge, somehow it was lost. The Universe is constantly expanding, along with the planets within galaxies, the place of origin of the Knowledge of the mind and its driving force, which is the planet that connects to all our minds.

You will discover the true meaning of The Holy Grail. It exists within us, enabling all to graduate to a new reality of existence by practicing a reality of freedom and love. This Knowledge grants us a unique perspective, which gives us the ability to understand numerous factors that were involved in bringing us to where we are today as a society.

On our journey to discovery we will also explore the true and unbreakable connection between our spiritual being and our physical bodies. There are billions of cells within our human structure. Several years ago, scientists, conducting a detailed study of the structure of our DNA, reported that humans have a very long, disconnected DNA strand in every cell. Within this DNA is a code that lies dormant. Our quest for truth will uncover the substance of that DNA. Encrypted in this life-code is The Holy Grail, which, you will soon learn, is Christ Consciousness.

Only the acknowledgment and initial implementation of Free will can give one access to the Knowledge and activate the disconnected DNA, resulting in total understanding and renewed connection between you and your soul (Higher self). The hidden secret to seeking our own purpose in this powerful, universal consciousness, begins and ends with complete love. When this is achieved, the lost encrypted code illuminates our energy, soaring to the highest dimensions of reality attaining "bliss." This will unite the two realms of existence back as one. Science is the missing link in our quest to exist in the unlimited realm of reality.

As Albert Einstein discovered in 1905, energy cannot be destroyed (Special Theory of Relativity). This energy has existed for all time. It fuels everything we create and see around us. The Universe is expanding rapidly, including all its galaxies, planets, moons and more.

What separates us from merely material creation as human beings, is our unique ability to create with our minds. Without the human mind, solely material creation would not exist. Material objects exist in a created experience of love. The element in which the object was created was formed from a vibration of love.

There are three elements of creation; the Universe's ability to expand, the galaxies within following the expansion, and the Mind of humans following the other two. If the mind exists in a reality not equal to the other two, ever-expanding entities, the reality in which we live will not align properly. Humans are missing the most important element of existence and purpose, which is existing in a reality strictly based out of love.

What the (Three Ages, will be defined in detail later) represented for the Mind was to bring to humanity the ability to create, out of the experience of love. All we perceive to be "real" only serves a materialistic system, designed solely by man, where only the material world is real, and love only exists as a form of commerce to obtain material things. These are false societal illusions.

The energy within all humans, both male and female, is the same. However, we are missing a vital part of our necessary experience while we are here. That missing element is unlimited love for each other.

For millennia we have existed in a limited reality of the experience of what love should be. Although it is difficult to accept, the fact remains that our planet was invaded by people from another galaxy in the Universe a very, very long time ago. From where exactly? I don't know. Yet, today, if we open our minds, we can understand why our governments have shielded us from the truth. Simply stated, aliens exist from beyond our planet. If the world's political leaders would verify that truth, it would lead to humanity beginning to understand that we really were invaded, causing our realities to be altered and compromised. These invaders appear like you and I, but their heartless acts identify who they are. Their intentions are the enslavement of our spirits through traumas, creating realities of fear and darkness.

Man has ruled renegade; outside of what is aligned with the energy of our reality. That energy is truly feminine, for as has been scientifically proven, the male embryo is female before it develops into the male gender.

This fact challenges the notion that we originated from a male creator. I believe we did not. We all are the offspring of this great energy. What separates us in the physical form is our gender. The energy within us is not limited to any race or gender. We are one body of energy from a loving energy of total bliss.

The heart and mind, together, were originally designed to be our own "imagineers"... creating all our desires. Our loving creator did not want the purposes of the two genders to become layered with false realities of darkness creating a limited environment. People must awaken to this truth now!

No human can create or own another human's physical life force. The Universe and its laws govern all beings. Our true source of creation, the highest level of energy, is manifest as a shimmering light, consisting of gold and white beams. The light represents Love and Gratitude. All humans are created with this identical energy. Every living thing shares this unique design of creation.

Humans harbor this energy within the spirit of their souls, which resides in their bodies in the realm of existence. My unique experience has convinced me that we are from a feminine energy. I understand that we harbor both male and female energies. Although my physical structure is fully female, my cells have recorded previous lives I led as both male and female. This explains my balance to both genders, and my understanding that they are of the same energy. To illustrate my personal discovery of this energy, common to us all, I recall vividly the following astral travel.

There came before me three humans: an African woman, a Chinese man, and a Caucasian man of unspecific ethnicity. I saw their detail, clearly. I was prompted to look at them through that shimmering light. I knew it to be the true source of creation, and I knew it to be Feminine. I saw the humans through this energy and they all were identical. I could not differentiate gender. The human's energy was of gold and white beams of light.

Our source of creation does not see hair, or eye, or even skin color. I realized that in every living thing, there is a vibration of energy that exists as one vibration. From this beautiful source we can act upon all our innate desires and understand how powerful we truly are.

It may seem far-fetched to believe that the energy of our mind has the power to create anything... by thought. However, I assure you that once the proper information has been practiced, showing how the mind functions and how Alchemy has a powerful connection, an individual can experience amazing results. One must perceive a completely new way to bring our knowledge of thought and existence together, enabling one to experience the world in the way it was always meant to be.

The limitations of humanity have stifled the mind from expanding into the Universe. The systems of limitation are based on greed by rewarding those who participate. The system does expand the mind, but not with the correct knowledge. Ultimately, each person who only existed in such a reality will discover at the end of their life cycle that they have been tragically fooled. The knowledge that will be explained in this book must be mastered while in the awakening consciousness.

The mind is like a free agent, receiving signals from the spirit. The spirit is connected to its soul within the Universe. Free Will is responsible for thinking and creating all things. Using our Free Will to harm, damage or destroy has led many people to settle for whatever is given by ruthless individuals. By not expanding our minds, we place all power in those ruthless individuals, organizations, and governments that create devastation, death, and destruction through chaos and war. This is mental enslavement of our unlimited power mind.

I believe the systems and institutions we have created have failed horribly. A great awakening is at hand.

The current physical and material realities are illusions. They are like holograms, an overlay on top of the true reality. To be able to live and thrive in this reality, it has been a requirement to learn economics, commerce (trade), and the realities of war. The experiences of limitation and fear have been the reality for many, in this dense, money-based existence. Missing in all is the one thing that is the most basic, most necessary element. That is love, above all else.

Our systems of government are designed to rob each person of valuable time, needed to reach the blueprint of the Holy Grail within the DNA of the soul. People are physically harmed daily over the illusion of obtainable value; ending their lives, removing them from their path to enlightenment, forcing them to experience another life cycle, to continue the journey to spiritual unity.

Wealth and material things reside in a false-value hierarchy, usurping our searching for the true reality created out of Love. We have been guided through our education to accept these values, without question.

It is essential that the reader comprehends that my knowledge has not been produced by any religious books. References to society's knowledge are mentioned, only to the degree of what is commonly known history, historical concepts, and personages. Organized Religion is what the invaders of man created. It caused the delay in awareness in growth and expansion. This book is not a religious tract. It is however, completely about "The Anointed One", Jesus Christ, and his continuing influence throughout our Universe. In later chapters you will discover Christ Consciousness and how we all can attain complete, permanent, spiritual unity through him, and him alone.

# NOTES

# 1

# EXPANDING THE MIND

Once we obtain the Knowledge that is within us, we can then use it to better our lives, those around us, and the natural environment. When enough people have done this, we can start to live as the powerful spiritual beings we are. If our minds are not expanding, nothing within our grasp can grow or change. The historical course of civilization will continue if we fail to understand this truth. When we are not expanding the mind, we remain trapped in a limited reality of beliefs created by those who desire to have us remain under their false version of reality.

When we understand and master all levels of our purpose and capabilities, we will no longer need to return to life on this planet, via reincarnation. Man created the reality we currently experience. It was not always this way. The Knowledge of how to create a better state of reality and living, was buried, purposely, and lost, a very, very long time ago. Earth continues to expand. Today it follows the Universe's path of constant expansion to accommodate all living organisms, including humans.

There are three cycles or "Perils" and are connected to three "Ages". To present day, there have been two previous perils. The Third Peril of Expansion is approaching. Many describe it Biblically as "The Rapture". That term frightens and intimidates me. I know it to be part of the religious control of thinking by our mental captors. It implies that our "sinning" will bring it to happen. This is a lie, a false tale. The Third Peril of Expansion has nothing to do with our mental actions, but instead, our physical consumption of elements. This expansion cannot be prevented or stopped by man or any other force, Not even Christ. This is the system of the Universe, and its laws . The planets expand, and our minds are to follow.

The forgotten cycles of consciousness are referred to as Ages: The Bronze, Silver, and the Golden. We are currently in the third, the Golden Age. This period allows the mind to build great structures, but only a selected group of minds have achieved this while all others have been limited by an undetected foreign force, closing many minds out of consciousness repeatedly, until the knowledge was forgotten, then buried. The previous Ages retain who we once were before any corruption of our minds occurred.

Many historians, modern and ancient, believe that there are really four Ages: The Golden, the Silver, the Bronze, and the Iron, in that order, leading to our present, modern age of man's designed reality. However, this is deceptive. The Iron Age is, in actuality, a false reality of mind control created through events that limit the mind

How did this come to be? Following the second Peril, as you will read in the upcoming chapter, our planet was invaded by an outside race of beings. They annihilated males while breeding with females to completely control our reality. They could not become ruler of man's consciousness though (This Is where Christ came in to save us all).

Today the offspring of the alien race incite chaos worldwide to undermine man's existence. Our reality is still in their grip. The difference between our species is fundamental. We, the non-alien, originated from love. The alien realizes that their control is slipping. Soon, men, women, and children will rise above their false implanted realities and see the path to the light of enlightenment and freedom.

The invaders can easily be identified. Who is in your presence that demonstrates ill intent? Who exists in a harsh reality by mistreating other humans, children and animals? We all have failed to see what motivates their actions. All of us are too busy fearing them instead of strengthening our own minds. We must understand their agenda, then work diligently to improve our reality. Because of their influence, the current reality has been limited, while this invading race has enjoyed our Knowledge in the present Golden Age. They practice our Knowledge, while enslaving our reality.

This Knowledge is still ours. We must realize it has been in our DNA. We must seek to find it. Our quest simply begins with a question... How deep is your love? Love is the most powerful and forgiving reality. Its power is manifest in all things.

We must rise above the darkness by reconnecting our minds to all three original Ages of Consciousness. These Ages involve the in-depth study of Love and Knowledge, without which our purpose for being here would be meaningless. These long, natural, universal cycles play a huge role in our ability to experience the powers of our soul, spirit, and mind, as an overarching, vibrational environment that surrounds us and permeates everything.

From my own Knowledge, gained through my travels on the astral plane, I have discovered that our Universe is expanding to accommodate all galaxies within it. I learned that the Bronze Age brought us an environment of enlightenment of love. The power of love will create the unwavering need for Knowledge that the Silver Age offers. The Silver Age consists of the in-depth study of Knowledge, including our ability to think and create. In the Silver and Golden Ages, we are fully aware of creation from a scientific perspective and simply know it. Then, the Golden Age yields to us the ability to manifest the elements and build enduring physical structures to make our collective mark in that unique cycle. The ability to use visualization and thought to aid in all our creations that will come. During the Golden Age, we realize there is no separation from the grains of sand, to the oceans tides, to the roaring volcanoes. We must think more of what should be, and not focus on what we think we are seeing and feeling. The ability to improve our reality is our passage out of this delusional purgatory. All energy is as one, including us.

As we carry the meaning and purpose of the Ages forward, we still carry with us the purpose of life – Love and Gratitude, specifically to feel and show Love and Gratitude to ourselves and to others. These are important for our well-being and spiritual growth. The sacred knowledge originates from our Universe, providing our galaxy with abilities to love, and create, while we are still growing.

# NOTES

# 2

# THE ALIEN MATRIX

Long ago, during Earth's Silver Age, an alien race invaded from another galaxy. They eliminated human males and began interbreeding with female humans. Their purpose was to create alien-human hybrids. This new sub-species would alter forever the inner workings of man's system of reality. This other-worldly intervention into the natural enlightenment of mankind is also known as the Dark Matrix.

Today, just as in ancient times, these beings entice, seduce, and force us to experience feelings of depression, despair, hatred, bloodlust, and more. This produces the energies they require to hold us in their false reality. Remember, they are part human. Many enlightened people continue to oppose the effects of this Dark Matrix.

The proliferation of guns and the true reason as to why high-powered AR-15's are available to citizens, mystify many today. But not me. Some believe it is to commit crimes against others. This is not the real purpose. The Dark Matrix is planning to repeat the bloody anarchies of the past.

I am not a gun owner. I am not opposed to people protecting their families, especially women and children. The ones who made this gun available did so to provide an opportunity for self- protection of the coming, non-military gun war. A war approaches against invaders who have been training on our turf, while learning to fly planes in our neighborhoods.

The invaders know exactly how to restart their influence when the Planet is close to self-destruction. We are not prepared for the upheavals of nature. Pandemonium will ensue. There are two contenders seeking control. One provides equipment to be obtained, while the other stages events, involving the controversial weapons to proclaim their danger to civilians. What they seek is little or no resistance to being overpowered and defeated. This is the truth behind it all.

The next event was the plan to use social media to influence elections. Mark Zuckerberg and his billion- dollar company were used expertly in the American Presidential election of 2016. Government investigations of the election would bring new laws sanctioning all social media. This means that certain material will be unviewable. The result will be to disallow parts of the world to be prepared.

The Dark Matrix aliens believe in their complete victory because they think that their intentions are deeply hidden. I can assure you they are not! This book will be available to every citizen. There are two types of people to resist the onslaught; The ones who are enlightened, and the ones who will not ever trust their government.

A practice of a certain reality causes all conflicts. The false reality created by the human-alien subspecies will no longer manipulate the humans of light. The events of centuries only serve to preserve their control until the next peril arrives. We must not fear the unknown of them. We stand collectively as strong energy full of love, and powerful hearts and minds!

The aliens and their hybrids no longer have a tight hold upon humans. Their Dark Matrix has weakened because they no longer have the power to impose their false reality upon us They are witnessing our access to the environments that enable our spirits to grow naturally. We have what is required. We have the capability to comprehend and remember that our reality has been changed and is not of man, causing many to accept everything they are taught, as true, without question. They fail to realize that it is the invaders writing false histories.

The "Anointed One's" life and message have been co-opted by the creators of untruths, misrepresenting what really occurred. This is how the aliens and hybrids gained compliance and trust from humans while imposing a false and dark reality.

Within the databases in our DNA, we have encrypted Knowledge to enable us to exist in a totally different reality. To achieve what we really are will require focused thought and committed action. Currently in our memories are only a few, basic details from previous life-cycles, such as our need to seek shelter. Intrinsically, we know to not live in the elements. By species memory, we automatically desire shelter. We also desire the sophisticated technology that will soon be government-regulated.

We know that technology makes our lives easier. Yet, our original, true knowledge has not been taught to society. It is difficult to recall what is correct, unless something helps the truth to surface. Many, like me, experience a great sense of knowing that there is something different about ourselves compared to others. It was a grand purpose in the shadows of the false reality.

For those who are working on behalf of the source creator and the "Anointed One", always know you are not alone. We are working on the same side. Together we will prevail against the darkness. We know the key is to forgive all and love all, no matter what. The darkness requires our fear and our hatred. Neutralize those emotions by forgiving and giving love. The darkness will recede, as it can't exist in the light of a beautiful reality. It can only survive in a reality of dark thoughts, and fear.

The purpose of this writing is to trigger something in you and bring the encrypted Knowledge to the surface of your reality now! The Darkness following the Second Peril yielded the swift act to preserve the ancient Knowledge, before the invader colony arrived in the ancient past. We were at our weakest point because our senses were becoming duller, and our minds less acute. The Universe was expanding.

At precisely that moment, a benevolent alien force, unlike the Dark invaders in every way, helped us, by building ancient structures. Among those created were The Pyramids of Giza. They were precisely aligned with the three Suns of Orion. Many parts of the planet where other cultures existed, also contained Pyramids. Their existence is to stand as constant reminders for future generations to not lose the sacred knowledge.

Many civilizations experienced great trauma by the recording of events of being pushed out of consciousness. The women and children were spared and became slaves, retaught to practice and exist in a reality of darkness. Our men pushed out of consciousness would be reborn to protect the women and children from these invaders of darkness. The period of awakening and enlightenment would return.

The rulers of civilization kept whatever Knowledge they had retained, while giving the people false stories and false histories through religion. The children became slaves to the invaders. As children grew to adults, any who demonstrated signs of the forbidden Knowledge were exterminated. This explains why so many cultures, such as the Mayans, disappeared from the planet.

Today, it is clear to see the reason that parts of Africa have been in ruins for so long. The indigenous people living there have held the Knowledge closest to our celestial home. They were the first creations of human life. They were the first to practice Love and Gratitude in The Bronze Age. Their unique physicality permitted them to endure the intense energy of the Sun. I knew as a child that there was something uniquely special about the African culture.

Their greatest purpose is Love and Gratitude. They started the Bronze Age. Because they endured two Ages and two Perils, they have a collective, cultural mind- strength realized in love, not darkness. Their culture has suffered unjustly, suggesting that they are deliberately singled out, not because of the skin color, but their ability to exist in a proud, but powerful, reality. It is a reality based on Universal laws of the higher self. It is a reality that has not been broken.

Africans taught the Egyptians the great knowledge and powers of the unlimited mind. During the Silver Age there were cultures existing in limited realities outside of the Egyptian civilization. The Jewish culture existed in limited reality. Their entry into Egypt was by invitation of the Pharaoh. History shows that It was the seer Joseph who requested his people be permitted to enter Egypt to escape famine.

The Jews were taught by the Egyptians to be craftsmen and merchants. Some 300 years would pass before Moses would be born to lead his people to safety due to the expansion of the planet Earth. This was the Second Peril, explained erroneously in the Bible as Exodus.

The event that caused Egypt to be overtaken by the "plagues" of numerous bugs and amphibians is akin to Moses leading the Jews from Egypt. The infestations and the fleeing were to save lives; human and animal, seeking higher ground as the Earth erupted, flooded, and changed.

Simply stated, there is no truth to the notion that the Jews were enslaved by the Egyptians. By the Jewish migration to Egypt, they escaped famine and death. That act of preservation did not bring about slavery. They integrated into the Egyptian world and learned new skills and crafts. Also, and most importantly, they learned Knowledge of life and reality from the Egyptians.

Moses knew this teaching. It was Knowledge traceable to African culture. He knew that he was to teach his people and share the Knowledge with the world. The Biblical "40 years" of wandering was time needed to learn the Knowledge. Without understanding its purpose, while under Roman rule hundreds of years later, Jewish priests began sharing the Knowledge with their Roman occupiers, with catastrophic results.

In time, the empire of Caesar would annihilate the Egyptian world and its connection to the Higher Realm. Darkness reigned throughout the land for hundreds and hundreds of years. The world cried out for salvation and hope. The era of "The Anointed One" was at hand.

He was known to possess the Knowledge of all the Ages. No one doubted his power to manifest miraculous events in an instant. They witnessed his insight. They heard him speak. They could feel his heart and his unlimited mind. He was a man beyond their meager capabilities.

The rulers, both in Rome and Jerusalem, could only enslave the reality of the mind by instilling control, fear and limitation. They knew he would challenge everything their power had brought to them. "The Anointed One" was captured, beaten, crucified and pushed out of consciousness or so they hoped.

Prior to the birth, life, and death of Jesus of Nazareth, the human spirit, after physical death, would eventually reincarnate, but under the rule of darkness. The "Anointed One's" first breaths meant the end of our spirits being lost in that dimension for eternity. The ultimate irony for The Sanhedrin, Pilate, Herod, and the mob who cheered his martyrdom is that Christ's final passion at Golgotha started a new consciousness for us all.

Our savior had finally come. As our lives ended, we were finally freed from the darkness in this realm of existence. In time, during the rule of Constantine, Christianity would become an organized religion to preserve the truth. Eventually, however, that truth would become corrupted and manipulated by those who saw the potential of control and power over the believers.

While the Knowledge became subjugated and abandoned by the institutionalized faith, likewise, the remnants of Judaism continued to slip further into a false reality of darkness. Some 400 years later, the Muslim religion was formed by an offspring of Jacob. How ironic that a descendant of Abraham, who rejected the "Anointed One", would begin a religious movement that is anathema to the life of Jesus Christ.

Centuries later, this and other man-made, religious institutions would continue the dogma of limiting Knowledge. They would also be complicit in sanctioning the inherent evils of slavery. The enlightenment of the Ages and Knowledge lived in the cells of tribes in Africa. They were systematically captured and enslaved. The irony, today, is clear. What darkness this era of enslavement brought to the world, ultimately has brought the demise of these institutions of control and limitation. Recall that The African was the first creation of human life, enduring through two full cycles of Ages. They were and are the strongest of humans. These powerful, enlightened beings were bought and sold worldwide, spreading their energy and knowledge.

My purpose is a part of that vibrant, African culture. My white skin does not speak to my vivid, past lives. We all exist in numerous disguises. What is inside, is not what you always see on the outside. Who we are, in truth, is not our shade of skin, but what lies deep within our cells.

It was meticulously planned that the Knowledge would become co-opted by society's enslavers. These religions filled lives with worshiping false events and gods. The Africans were viewed as ignorant and savage. Once it was discovered what they held within their cells of reality, they were singled out and tormented. When it was understood that they would not become compliant, they were cast into deprivation. Their enslavement would last for many centuries. Their strength held strong.

Today, all Africans and other cultures of light must take their place in spreading their beautiful purpose to all. They must follow "The Anointed One" precisely to his methods. They must spread the knowledge to all people. They must forgive what has been done in the past. It has been a very long journey. Progress is being made. Most peoples of the world are not physically enslaved, as centuries ago. Today we must focus solely on our realities.

The past programming of the mind must be dealt with while alive in this consciousness. Striving to reconnect our minds to the previous Ages of time, will deliver us to the present Age, The Golden Age. This Knowledge will be in all corners of the world, resulting in love, peace, and harmony. It is our greatest purpose. Only then shall we emerge onto the path of eternal freedom and the "Anointed One", will return. The time has arrived to reconnect to the previous reality we all knew quite well.

The systems that create the reality of limitation, are finally being dismantled. They include the intelligent and applied minds of society, such as global planners and scientists. Many of these people are well known. They have hoarded the Knowledge, Earth's resources, and Mankind's treasure. They have successfully kept humanity in ignorance. By creating false histories and religions, fabricating false events (events that happened differently than presented, or which had a different purpose than stated), they have made people believe untruths about themselves, the world, the universe, and the intentions of world leaders.

Before the first quarter of the 21st century is completed, astrophysicists and engineers are planning Earth colonies on the planet Mars. What if there are other beings already there? What I have written of us being invaded is now not a farfetched notion. The missions to Mars are really preparation for the next Peril of Expansion. If there are intelligent beings on Mars, I fear they will be corrupted by the colonizers. The dark forces that have cloaked our reality and controlled this planet may spread their dark venom there too.

The beings that invaded this planet can be found in all levels of Government around the world. Many are high ranking religious leaders, who have kept their bloodline pure by taking multiple wives, producing many children with many half siblings. They avoid the chromosome nightmare by keeping with their peculiar mating system. The same father with multiple mates produce children. Those children may interbreed with cousins on their father's side without the often-found side effects of inbreeding. Outside blood-lines are never allowed to mix with their bloodline, due to the cell imprints of limitations that have been imprinted upon most spirits of society, which creates the current reality. This means that the bloodlines of ruling families experience a different reality than most of us do. They do not participate in the same reality. They manipulate and create the master reality of limitation of fear, keeping their subjects in turmoil and conflict.

Our realities are programmed by the realities of darkness that have enslaved us. Because we believe the programming to be real, we embrace it. Once we can reach enlightenment, we can begin to free ourselves of this programming. Liberating ourselves from this programming may be a multi-life process, involving ascension to a higher dimension at each stage of progress. I believe that our suffering and hard work of the past is bringing positive results. I envision all ages of people reaching their total heights of reality. It is all about energy and the power of the minds, and hearts connecting as one.

If we will realize it, our minds continue to open and expand. This often involves remembering one or more past lives. Reconnecting to the knowledge of the past can help us detect the falsehoods of our programming. This awareness can help us understand the answers are already within us. My intentions are to help others improve their reality by encouraging critical thinking and loving as a practiced reality instead of what has been practiced.

The key to achieving ascension to the highest realm of reality, while in the conscious state of life, is to experience all the good we can imagine, and love to the fullest in this current consciousness. Our emotions and powerful vibrations will steer the outcome by sending signals of energy to our Soul. Consequently, that valuable energy sends its unique pattern to the "ether" (that unseen substance upon which all is written) and is used by the Universe to create the desire you have expressed with your thought.

The soul is only connected to acts of love. Anything other than love is the force of darkness. In response, the ether then delivers a series of exact events to you, a kind of serendipitous effect, which is determined by the type of energy that you, through your intention and vibration, manifest. Most of the realities we have experienced throughout multiple life cycles of the ages have been designed to keep us from the truth and further instill in our minds the concepts of limitation and fear. This conflicts with what is needed for us to exist in a reality of light, because when we embrace limitation and fear, we often behave in ways that produce more darkness, such as controlling or dominating someone else to feel more powerful, either by boosting us or limiting the other person. Our participation creates the plight of the ones who must overcome the ones who create and control the reality.

Too many times, we are faced with false, misleading, or missing information in our pursuit of purpose. Spiritual acknowledgment plays a key role in progressing through proper steps that are necessary to complete all that we must master and own from the present life cycle.

The proper steps include understanding the science of who and what we are, and the science of creating with our mind. We must also acknowledge that the "complete us," from the depths of who we are, is pure energy or pure love. We must fully grasp that the most powerful piece of equipment our source creator ever engineered and created is the mind of our soul and spirit, that brings forth all we could ever imagine, by the powerful vibration of love from the heart.

The heart is the most powerful source of vibration. Emotions of love created by the heart produce the strongest vibration, when manifesting our desires according to the creation process. This is also the extension of the love of a feminine energy in all created universes.

At the end of our spiritual journey, we will have reached the highest realm possible in our existence. This plateau is Love and Gratitude. Material possessions are irrelevant. Love and Gratitude are the only experiences that allow every spirit to graduate to the Knowledge of Christ consciousness and the Higher Realm of our purpose and existence.

This has always been the Truth and the Agenda. We create wealth and draw the things we desire to us using natural universal laws, not man's system of physical reality. What a huge misconception we have lived under. The invaders' reality keeps us seeking and consuming more and more material items.

The only way to earn the acceptance of the Higher Realm is to own the Knowledge we have had the entire time. Free will, as I define the term, means an activation of the mind toward gaining Knowledge, helping one achieve advancement to a Higher Realm of understanding, and toward creating specific experiences guided by love. It means to "free" the will of the soul and use the mind to create experiences by the loving guidance of the heart.

Exercising one's Free Will leads to being able to exercise complete freedom. The opportunity to experience and learn how Free Will works begins with exercising ordinary laws, by making choices, without threat or persecution from any other party, having the freedom to think and act, providing that one commits no violations against another. It is imperative to have the freedom to act and create – but this freedom does not include the right to harm another living being. Indeed, this is the only lawful limitation. Those who harm others or the planet for their own agendas have not accepted this limitation, and therefore, act outside of universal Law.

Throughout history, there have been many devastating acts carried out by the invaders that continue to interrupt the vibration of love. These dark acts impact our minds by robbing our bliss, separating us from the truth. Against their greatest efforts, I truly believe they are ultimately failing. I know that the vibration of love is stronger than ever before. I see great progress. We no longer exist as before. We are rising to a stronger reality and understanding. I see tremendous compassion for all living things, from all ages and cultures. It is a beautiful gift to us all to witness this while being a part of this grand event!

The invaders, from their earliest arrival, have influenced the world's leaders by using physical force to create the reality they desired. This ensured their success in continuing the separation from where most of us originated, and from us knowing what is real.

Fortunately, as I write, the winds of change are beginning to blow. We are no longer allowing ourselves to be controlled or limited by others for their purpose and agenda, we are seeking the understanding of the hidden Knowledge of the soul, realizing that the spirit has been trapped in this false reality of doom. We are claiming back our natural birth rights.

The actions and motives of the Dark Matrix are more visible and obvious than ever. Their actions are what separates them from us. Recall the recent statements of inventor Elon Musk. They support a past timeline of events of total and true accuracy to succeed to make it to Mars. Who will be the chosen colonists? It clearly appears that events are being planned right now for the next Peril, and the planned attack on society by an army from the Middle Eastern Army that they are building.

Consider the intriguing Denver Murals. These works, from Chicano artist Leo Tanguma, are interpreted by some as depicting children of the world, abandoned by missing parents. Those young people illustrate the candidates for transport to Mars. The darkness that invaded here will use our technology, resources, and children to move to the next planet. They eventually want to colonize the entire Universe with darkness. I am not implying that Elon Musk is alien, yet he is working under their direction and purpose. A person of such intelligence is not ignorant to the fact of how the reality is being controlled and what is coming.

I know that many scientist or global planners are being influenced and led by working on behalf of the Dark Matrix. Their knowledge and achievements in hi-tech, solar, satellites and more, are used against society. Nicola Tesla was a pioneer in electrical technology. His hope was for it to be a free, worldwide resource. Do you think he was controlled by them? Absolutely not!

In December 8, 2000, I had the awakening to what has been done to us all over thousands of years. Today I understand how simply all humankind can thwart their attempts to trap us in their purpose. It is our minds and spirits that are enslaved, because of false beliefs of untrue stories.

We must realize and understand that we are racing against time, and that our planet is on a course of destruction that cannot be prevented or stopped. However, we can become enlightened in our minds and free our spirits by practicing a reality that will yield us the right to return to our original form, when our life cycle is complete. To remain in a realm of wholeness, we must change how we are existing right now.

An important step in this necessary change is understanding the science of astral travel. It is crucial to the discovery of true Knowledge. We all have this knowledge, even if we are unaware of its existence. Prior to the Dark Matrix control, we all traveled back to our souls during each resting cycle. We would awaken in this reality, only to be lost when our reality was altered.

While in our waking hours, we witness chaos and suffering at all levels. This alters our cells of experience. Our spirits are weighed down with fear and limitation. However, when we sleep, our spirits try to break free from this dark cloud. Many times, we believe we are sleeping, when in fact our vessel (body) has settled into a relaxed and unconscious mode, while the soul's spirit is reviving, preparing to take flight. attempting to reconnect. However, out of fear, we hover below, trapped, fearing to travel through matter. The courageous spirits do travel through matter, seeking answers. For those who exit through matter, what they recall as dreams, are real to their spirit. This could be why we have déjà vu experiences. When this happens, it simply means that your soul's spirit is ahead of what is coming, in your experience, in this reality. Only in this reality do we count time. In the Higher Realm, timekeeping does not exist. In astral travel, we can go forward and backward in time.

The subconscious mind exists outside of time. The spirit can revisit the past and see the future before it happens. Once the experience arrives in the physical reality, the soul's spirit recognizes it and ensures that the ego and personality perceive it. The soul's spirit will guide the vessel by using superior Knowledge, as the spirit is connected to the Higher Realm, always through the invisible energy of the soul.

The Higher Realm influences us while we sleep, hoping that we will astral travel, seek the true Knowledge, and help us avoid potential danger. This innate skill in each of us cannot be sanctioned, prevented, or changed by anyone, human or alien. The government cannot check your spirit to find out where it has been, nor prevent it from going where it wills. When all people realize this, they will know that they are no longer limited by borders or passports. We are capable of such travel, even into space without material craft. I know, I have traveled to space twice with my energy. I send the energy of thought to all people to choose to go where their energy can be taught the truth, and where the soul's spirit can record all Knowledge. No matter where the spirit goes in astral travel, remember that Knowledge is absolute power!

I cannot emphasize enough the importance of looking deeply and carefully at everything that is around us in the physical reality. Everything in the invaders' dark realm is a mirror image of themselves and an opposite, and an unreal reflection of our celestial home in the Universe. What is not mirrored is the reality we practice on purpose, and with Knowledgeable intent. We must bring our encrypted code to the surface of reality, forever rejoining both realms of spirit and soul.

We have been conditioned to believe that this reality is the only reality of existence. But it absolutely is not! Of course, this reality seems real, as we see it through our eyes, and we feel it with our bodies, and our hearts weep with sadness at the suffering. History has been altered to perpetuate a false reality.

My writings help others free their minds. I believe that religions should represent the absolute truth. The faithful should feel love and freedom. Instead we see the promotion of hatred and prejudice, creating a limited reality of existence.

Today the two religions based out of one culture of people from Abraham (Judaism and Muslim) are carrying within them the Egyptian knowledge extended to Joseph and Moses. Today the two religions, but same bloodline are fighting to rule the world's reality through life consciousness, before the next Peril. They have dominated by successfully placing limits on societies by controlling the minds around them and the elements of resources in the region, creating a reality that supports their agenda. Many fail to see the constantly repeated patterns throughout history. Religion has served a dark agenda of Lucifer, not the purpose of the "Anointed One".

We are enabling this reality by embracing their dogma. This is about the mind of reality not the physical body. We must not fail to rise above the ignorance we have been taught over centuries.

We must learn to think in a reality of love. There is no substitution that can make us whole again. Only knowledge of "The Anointed One" and his love, peace, and unity will bring the change in all of us.

## REVEALED KNOWLEDGE

▲ The Mind holds all the answers and solutions to all realities each person exists in while in the present time. The reality we embrace and practice becomes our existence.

▲ The Mind helps create the reality of existence by the cells located within the energy the DNA.

▲ Every human can think, change, and create new paradigms to replace the old cells. This is done by constant repetition. Society doing this together is key to returning order to our existence.

▲ The Mind will naturally resist, but the experience of fear should come as a relief because it is part of the new transition.

▲ As time passes and progress is made, the cells will grow and the encrypted codes of Knowledge will push through. Eventually, fear will be difficult to recall.

▲ The powerful Mind will draw from the library within us. Be patient and reassure your powerful thoughts. They will strengthen and signal a strong vibration into the Cosmos in due time.

▲ Coming back is a journey. Pay close attention and keep a journal, if possible. Once you have removed the layers of man's deceit, it will be difficult to recall the fear and ignorance because the system has taken on a whole new form.

- ▲ This is birth Knowledge and can never be removed.
- ▲ Time is of the essence to raise the consciousness.
- ▲ Each person must separate man's system from this Knowledge.
- ▲ Man's system enslaves, but the encrypted Knowledge creates freedom.

# NOTES

# 3

## THE SUPERIOR POWER OF THIS UNIVERSE

Our minds interact with the Universe in a very real and profound way. The science behind our complex mind allows it to harbor many amazing gifts of superior Knowledge. These gifts remain dormant, yet are waiting to be rediscovered by each of us. The vast number of receptors located throughout our bodies have been reacting to the wrong system of information. This bogus and harmful data, taken into the mind and brain, creates erroneously programmed cells that comprise our current environment and reality. The result is devastating. It leaves a dark void in our hearts. The mind and the body are always ready to be fired up and used in a productive way for the benefit of all species of energy (all beings). This connection to the Universe is the energy of our purpose.

Each of us possesses the ability to harness the energy in and around us. Once the Knowledge has been learned and utilized in a way that will enlighten the heart, the reality in which we have existed will improve to the ultimate understanding. We can then begin the journey home to our natural, macrobiotic state of mind. We will also begin to understand the vibration of this planet, and how energy cannot be created or destroyed, no matter how many times we experience what we know as life and death.

Death is not real! Please comprehend this!

Many believe that because we cannot see our loved ones, they no longer exist. This could not be further from the truth. I understood this truth after I ascended to the Higher Realm nearly eighteen years ago, after suffering a near-death experience. Death is a false paradigm. It is a temporary, transitional state of existence, not the end of our being. We will always exist within our Universe as energy, unto eternity. We cannot ascend to the Higher Realm until we have been processed through a buffer in the astral plane of reality, when all things will become known and understood. There we connect to the Reality of the Higher Realm. True Knowledge must be achieved and realized from within us while we are in this powerful consciousness of existence. When that occurs, we may graduate to a higher level of understanding, before we return to the higher dimensions.

The true beginning of our current reality and existence will soon be revealed. Humanity is much older than we have been taught. Our reality has been under a false existence for thousands of years. We all have forgotten this information due to our current practices and beliefs. If the required Knowledge is not mastered in this powerful reality of consciousness, by the time of our cycle ending, we are sent back to this realm for another physical life. Without self-discovery, we eventually fall into the same traps of enslavement of the soul's spirit. Each life cycle can render more layering of the false reality. This makes it difficult to remember any progress of the previous life cycle, if any at all was made.

We cannot remember or relearn any of the true Knowledge on our own, because of our programming and the elaborate schemes and tricks that are practiced by the facilitators of this reality of illusion. Knowledge removed and prevented from being known has enabled their false reality to exist for many thousands of years. Divine intervention throughout the ages has kept this message of Truth alive, but its meaning has been obscured and corrupted. Until we improve our reality and seize complete control of our destiny and Knowledge we remain separated from the truth. We must understand that we are female and male, created by a beautiful energy source. We are created in its likeness, capable of learning all that is required to live and exist in a reality of Bliss and Love and Gratitude.

Many events over the past decades are systematically being erased from all traces of our other celestial existence. Historical truths are being obscured and reinterpreted. Humans are callously violating other humans. Is there no way to stop this gradual elimination of moral and ethical consciousness?

This dimming of our path to the true light of reality is necessary now. It is in advance of the Third Great Peril of Expansion, following the expanding Universe and the inertial force that it creates. It is a pulling force, affecting all galaxies and any other celestial bodies. In the Second Peril, during the time of the Biblical Exodus, all knowledge was purposely destroyed. That devastating pattern is now repeating.

When this coming Peril eventually subsides, a new existence of more planned limitations will rule. To succeed, an overall dismantling of Law is occurring. The romantic notion of being a rebel or a crusader will be purged from history. No living society of humankind will be spared.

The late writer, professor, and comparative religion expert, Joseph Campbell, did an outstanding job researching the world's religious/mythological origins. His findings, interestingly, shared many similar patterns. For instance, "A son is born to a virgin, to be man's savior." This explains how the Higher Realm has continued to return order to the collective human consciousness.

The purpose of war and the tools of war serve to drive many out of this consciousness, before discovering what is required of them. This deadly "reality game" eliminates many people prior to their understanding of the true reality. The invaders bring disease and pestilence to the minds and hearts, keeping many soul-less.

When the truth is rediscovered, we will see how simple and natural and beautiful it is, always there for us to find. As the vibration of the "Anointed One" is felt, we absorb the Knowledge. The "Anointed One's" bliss accompanies us into the Higher Realm.

The blueprint for this system of reality on Earth, will have little effect on the lives of the next generation of children. They are merely souls pushed out in previous times by numerous acts or situations. The future child will be reborn carrying the "Anointed One's" Holy Grail. Their vibration of reality will serve to mirror the child's reality of love, truth and unity. That essence is instilled by Christ himself. Our reality will become one with the children, who are the loved ones returning to experience and finally understand their true purpose. Who would not desire to do all possible to ensure our loved ones are spared from existing in a reality any less glorious.

Our efforts will help our parents, children, and all others in achieving enlightenment. I am so excited to see that future child, experiencing all the wonder and Knowledge in each of us.

Universal Laws govern all things in our temporary existence on Earth. Because of our Free Will, we must use these rules to exist differently while in this consciousness. Our reality can be improved by loving and forgiving those who have harmed us, while not judging others for their behavior. Once we live, day-by-day, following those tenets, the Higher Realm will assist and light our path.

Our present, limited reality causes us to behave opposed to our true selves. The concept of material wealth had long troubled me. I believed it to be partly responsible for the suffering in the world. Eventually, however, I realized that wealth as an abstract, is not responsible for the suffering it has wrought. Many on the thrones of world power have performed acts that appear brilliant and inspired, while in fact, many, but not all, have achieved their level of material wealth by acts of dishonesty, deceit, and manipulation.

Because the world is always "for sale", the corrupt ones have a free pass to behave without penalty. They never experience their true purpose. They are unaware of its existence completely. Their acts continue to cloud and darken our lives. They are grossly enslaved to this reality. Upon their return to the Higher Realm after death, they cannot enter their own soul because their cells and vibrations are too inadequate. They reincarnate into their next lives, drawn to the same experiences that had been recorded in their previous life. They are ignorant of the fact that their own cells are vibrating them to the same repetitive experiences that trap and enslave them again and again. They remain unaware of their bondage. They continue to believe in their superiority. They must return to make corrections in their own limited reality

Regardless of their actions, we must take control of our own reality and do what is necessary to build the strongest foundation while we still can. Time is very short. The evil planners and controllers are planning a mass extermination, specifically of men, before the Third Peril. This heinous slaughter will continue the practice of what has been for multiple thousands of years.

As babies are reborn, and show Knowledge of the last Age, they will be eliminated also. The act to separate mothers from their children has occurred in the past, and still is today. In a prior life, I was a child who was separated from my mother and pushed out of consciousness, in the beginning of The Golden Age. I recall vividly shouting "This is not how it is supposed to be!"

I know their tactics well. Only one who knows can write such truth. Regardless of what is coming, what we harbor in our cells is vitally important. Once the energy releases from the physical realm, a beautiful knowledge will fill the Universe with love! We must master loving each other so much!

There are two important truths I need to master; the science of Alchemy, advancing the mind to master the ability to create wealth of knowledge that leads to material achievements, and, the art of communication and its purpose, relating to my purpose for writing such knowledge. To practice the original method of limitless thinking is to create a reality that reveals the higher self. Universal laws react to our mind, our vibration and our love. The intention of the heart must be aligned with those laws.

We must separate from the methods and practice of the invaders of man. Their purpose only serves to encourage chaos. No human or alien can ever own this planet. When the mind is free of influence of their tactical diversions, it is clear to see there is far more to their agenda than the controlling of our natural resources. What they prize most is the control of our individual and collective consciousness. When that is fully understood, you will begin to grasp the absolute importance of my message.

We must take off the blinders and see beyond our time-worn traditions and practices. Who really believes that existing in our present reality is correct? Our questions are many. Where did we come from? How did we learn? Where are we returning to? Are we originating from chaos, only to return to another dimension of reality that is the same as what we experience here in this consciousness of life?

I fully comprehend that we ascend to a beautiful realm of existence. I know, I have the ability to retrieve data through my own cells, that recorded the experiences of my past lives. I recall each return to a perfect realm. I was outside of the false reality and consciousness. I saw the traditions we are all taught, and how our participation in them causes the separation. It once robbed us of our purpose, but no longer.

I know that wealth is not limited solely to money or material possessions, as most think of it. True wealth includes the richness of our soul. The most important wealth is love, leading to material creation. It is never to sway us from our abilities to know how to create all we desire.

Most indulge in this practice of seeking wealth, not realizing the system which the invaders of man created, usually involves loans and obtaining credit scores. The system is designed as it is, but it is each person's Free Will that embraces it.

We teach our children by example. Many children raised in poverty remain in poverty. This perpetuates the system and how it exists in a limited reality. There are also children, born in poverty, who grow to become wealthy. This proves they returned under a challenge, and still achieved what was recorded in previous experiences. What was recorded previously in the cells will vibrate to the same experience. This is a fact of our unlimited abilities to exist in what we are drawn to by what we unknowingly know.

How does this happen? There are two life cycles that can be chosen. One is to serve a great purpose, such as returning to live a new experience. A spirit who existed in a previous life may choose to return to experience a life of poverty. One may ask but why? There is a simple answer. These spirits are returning specifically to become an example that poverty is a choice, within a state of mind.

Acquiring the Knowledge does not require a formal college education. To the contrary, college serves to continue the system of history of reality created by the dark matrix. All concepts and programs that were hatched from the network of this bloodline group of invaders and hybrid rulers are responsible for our current reality, through the manipulation of history, nations, and leaders. The system they created, which we all inherit at birth and then must overcome, has served the purpose of ensuring that this false reality survives as the reality in which we exist and live. Their idea of college replaces our required knowledge of the Universe and our higher purpose of existence.

There is no Knowledge superior to the Higher Realm. It flows through us to activate our Free Will, and utilize the natural energy of our universe to improve our reality. Only superior Knowledge creates superior wealth, and where the creation of all things begins.

We have all been taught that a collegiate education is part of our purpose. Watching the popular television quiz show "Jeopardy" recently, I was struck by this observation. The show features contestants who are quite intelligent in the histories of time of the practiced reality, over decades and centuries. But, I have not witnessed anyone speaking of the Knowledge that I write about. I don't believe studying a reality, within the same reality, makes anyone intrinsically smart.

My visions of the patterns of the past occur during my hours of sleep. I experience surreal events, not only involving me, but others. We have been taught that the only true reality is the one we can see and are awakened in, what we can touch, or experience in our physical waking hours, "The physical reality". This is a falsehood in our minds. It portrays us as powerless and weak. It describes us as incapable of original thought and incapable of making rational decisions.

As my energy became alchemized and I could escape the vessel that housed it, along with this reality, I realized I had been traveling to the

Higher Realms, a protected dimension of reality. I truly experienced these events. I was not merely dreaming. I am confident in knowing that the "Anointed One" was present in my spirit and mind, guiding me back to his reality. My ability to astral travel, and the times I visited him in the Higher Realm, while living in this current false reality, are real experiences of my life.

This was crucial in my research; explaining how I had so much intuitive Knowledge, although, I had yet to pick up a book that referenced such Knowledge. I had the innate ability to see the chaos and recognize the cause. From childhood forward, we are taught to revere the power of those who rule the land. We are further indoctrinated in the tenets of their falsely created religions. Each are merely tricks and diversions from their true purpose and focus. All the subterfuge hides their desire to control the consciousness of humankind.

As the life cycle of us all is only spent participating and reacting to the traditions of what should not ever have been, we discover how easy it is to be tricked by the system. Man does not have the power to cause anyone to think or exist in any way. We all have Free Will and we participate because the correct way is hidden and suppressed. We do have memory. We can quickly recall images of catastrophe, doom, and death. These are necessary triggers to keep emotions of fear, hatred and revenge vibrating from our hearts.

Something, however, has happened. People are not reacting in revenge. Instead, they are pleading for peace. They are learning the power of forgiveness. Our original, first-natures are still there, yet masked by the darkness. The horrid acts we witness daily are not from our source of creation. They are the craven acts of an invading fleet, appearing as you or I, creating situations that are affecting the world, less and less.

When this spiritual quest began for me, I felt a great weariness throughout my body. My soul's energy (my spirit), was leaving my body and traveling to so many places, I had no idea what was going on. Finally, I realized that the "Anointed One", Christ, was not the only spiritual being to talk to me in-depth about alchemy of the energy that leads to astral projection and out-of-body experiences.

I recall on two separate occasions, being awakened by my cat Serenity, jumped onto the bed, while I was having an out-of-body experience. I recall my body feeling the sensation of my essence, my spirit, returning. Wow! This was proof positive that I was leaving my body while my body was in rest mode. What an amazing experience it was, to be awake as my energy returned to its physical vessel. As I descended back to my body by means of my life-line, my vortex, a silvery transpersonal antenna that records all experiences and keeps my spirit attached to my vessel, staying connected to me while I soar to wherever I want to go, I realized immediately that I did not want to return to this reality, in this consciousness. It was such freedom and it felt so natural. I was napping every chance I possibly could to have this experience of freedom, knowing my cells are constantly recording all experiences. In this state of consciousness, you are not limited to where you can go or what you can do. It may not seem like it. But, our consciousness is improving and connecting back to its original form.

Our energy can travel through walls, windows, doors, fire, water, and even solid stone. I found myself defying the laws of physics with every natural rule broken, once I realized I had been doing this for the eternity of my existence as an offspring of my very own creator and source. This discovery also supports and proves to me that there are two parts to "Alchemy:" one is seen (physical) and the other is the experience, invisible energy, (The Spirit). One cannot exist without the other. I understand that our energy is limitless. Nothing can prevent a spirit of consciousness from experiencing and learning, while alive in the flesh.

This is precisely what the Egyptians practiced. They understood and freely used Alchemy and the ability to travel through matter. Once I realized where and how I acquired my Knowledge, I paid closer attention.

This is a crucial aspect of our Knowledge and path of consciousness. It is being reunited with the natural Source of Knowledge and energy of our brilliance. Because of it, I could see, in this present consciousness, the required Knowledge that will save our soul's spirit in this current reality, the Knowledge that will allow us to transcend, so that we can stop coming back for lessons.

How do we ascend to the Higher Realm?

We must use our mind to discover the reality that harbors the Knowledge. That which we have believed to be real, we have allowed to enslave our soul's spirit. The acquisition of this Knowledge is necessary before we can free ourselves from the current reality that compels us to want and fear while promoting ignorance. Our priority, then, is to return to our soul with this Knowledge. We must do so to be whole again. Those who fail to learn this Knowledge within the current reality will face another life-cycle where chances to learn what is required will deteriorate drastically (By erasing Christ from reality).

Many have been conditioned to believe, and act upon the belief, that hard labor brings material wealth. In some cases, this is true, but the mind is far more capable of creating wealth, at a faster pace, than any manual labor. Many have worked their bodies to the bone, pursuing wealth inside the system created by the invaders, where humans are required to pay a wealthy elite for the "privilege" of living on a planet that cannot and will not be owned by anyone.

The laws of the invaders of man, in the past and the present, demonstrate the ignorance and weakness of human man. These manmade laws, where a privileged elite control and oppress the rest of the population, stand in direct conflict with Universal Law. It is our birthright, our inalienable right, to be governed only by the creator's source energy, which is our source of existence.

After my death and recovery nearly two decades ago, a surprising self-discovery occurred. When I was twenty-three years old, I fully understood my ancient origin. I arrived here, on Earth, a very long time ago, before The Second Peril. It was proven to me that there has always been, and always will be, other realms of life beyond this planet. I know that I originated from a galaxy of light. It was one of many that was once adjacent to our Milky Way Galaxy.

I chose to come here to experience life in the flesh, while I also intended to protect the Knowledge from being forgotten and erased. I acquired this self-awareness, and you can as well. The other dimension of reality can make itself known to us, in this reality, through its connection to us through our cells, within our DNA. This allows our minds to be a kind of portal. Through it, we can remember what has already been before now.

The world from which I came, did not exist as today. There was not a controlling, invading force, cutting off our necessary communication, preventing us from learning what we truly are... Illuminations of Love. Blessedly, at long last, the dark reality is beginning to weaken. As more minds connect to the vibration of truth, the realities of those enlightened people are improving. While we strengthen our reality, the invaders control over us slowly lifts, as a great fog evaporates in the morning sun.

We truly are an infinite source of energy that can never be destroyed. Our energy has no limits. The way to create a whole reality of love has always been in us all. We must not fear seeking this existence. We must accept a reality of forgiveness, not judgement. We must seek the outcome of becoming a reality of love. This is what must be done to forever eliminate the created reality of our dark past.

# REVEALED KNOWLEDGE

▲ The cells in our body allow emotions to be experienced, recording of the past to improve the reality of our future.

▲ Think of all the emotions and scale them according to your own experience. If you feel the emotion of love the most, it is an indication than you harbor more love cells than any other. If you acknowledge fear or worry, you harbor within you the cells of fear or limitation. If you feel anger beyond words, you harbor the darkness of a combination of fear, hatred and revenge, which was man's reality that is no longer relevant.

▲ Emotions help us to recognize where we need to focus in order to improve and acknowledge what separates us from the truth.

▲ Often, the most practiced cells are connected to many past lives and are manifest as the existence while in the current consciousness.

▲ You can change and improve by utilizing your Free Will. Do not carry negative experiences throughout your life; they must be altered now before the cycle ends. Your cells must harbor the truth and carry great love back to your origins. The false reality must be eliminated while alive in the consciousness.

▲ Three key points: love, forgive, and do not judge anyone, no matter what they have done. Remember some have suffered tremendously at man's will. None of us are superior to the other.

▲ The goal is to avoid returning to repeat the same acts again through reincarnation. We must change and improve our reality of existence while we are here in the present consciousness.

# NOTES

# NOTES

# 4

# THE SCIENCE OF CELL INTERACTION IN THE VESSEL

The vibrations from our environment influence the cells in the human body. The level of vibration at which our bodies function depends upon how we comprehend our own environment and how that environment influences us to react. Do we live and act as light-spirited or dark-spirited humans? Do we provide energy by what may be our unique insight, or are we afraid to separate ourselves from the pack?

We manifest our desires by creating new experiences. We create new cells intrinsically aware of the science of Alchemy. Our energy inside of us reacts to outside energy. Our unique vibration is created. How we react is projected at that moment. The powers of experience, by pretending or otherwise, are awesome. Allow me to share a vivid example.

My apologies if anyone is offended by my choice of subject. I mean no disrespect to this well-known actor who tragically died in recent years. I only use his life experience to illustrate the mind's power, and its ability to translate an individual's thoughts into pure vibration, creating a reality.

Christopher Reeve was a famous, successful actor. "Above Suspicion" was his last movie before his life-changing accident. In the film, his character was a quadriplegic. Unfortunately, he played his role too well. To better understand the character, Reeve did an actor's research. He studied quadriplegics eight hours a day for eight months at a rehabilitation center. The more he rehearsed his part in his mind, the more he unwittingly fed the growth of the reality of a "quadriplegic". He was strengthening the cells with his mind. The more nourishment he gave these cells, the stronger the signal. Eventually, the vibration he was creating, reached the higher self, that this was to be his new reality and experience.

Merely pretending, in the present moment, will manifest whatever is desired. Repetition and intensifying focus lead to manifesting at a faster rate. His emitted thoughts created by his own mind were mirrored by the cells in his body engineered a new outcome, until the role he played led to his experience of a mirrored reality. I believe that if Christopher Reeve had known and understood this hidden knowledge, he certainly would have avoided the outcome.

The soul of us is the Universe within us all. It is what most refer to as "The Genie". This energy reacts to our desires. As we create the vibration of our desires, our Genie reacts and delivers to us both good and bad. How we exist creates the reality we experience. We each control the "magic lamp." We are the boss and creator of our own success or failure. All we experience must teach us great lessons to look beyond what we have practiced until now and see a true reality.

Only fear and limitation created by a false reality can prevent us from activating our Genie. Those roadblocks never interfered with Christopher Reeve. The world lost a loving and gifted person. We will always hold him dear to our hearts. Today, we recall his riding accident as an example of how powerful our minds truly are and have always been. The example of Christopher Reeve also shows us what can happen, when we don't comprehend the true science, or the infinite powers of our minds.

Though Reeve's body died, his spirit returned home to his soul with our source creationand the "Anointed One", our savior Christ. As I am writing, from my computer I hear the beautiful melody from his romantic film, "Somewhere in Time." I believe it's his way to nudge me. He is aware of my acknowledgement of him. From an amazing experience in my past onward, I have felt that he and I were truly connected.

That particular night, in 2012, during an astral journey, I had a profound encounter with Christopher in the astral realm. He spoke candidly to me saying (and I recall the words precisely!) "Hollywood had better wake up! Be careful who you have in your presence, their cells of reality can alter yours and influence you." He ended the encounter stating, as a matter of fact, the most shocking of the three things he spoke to me. "You and I were cousins sixteen generations ago!" I immediately woke up and wrote his messages down. Hours later, I called a friend who is a math whiz, and asked him how long is sixteen generations? He told me that it was three hundred and fifty years! I'm firmly convinced now that Hollywood is waking up, finally, from the mind control and exploitation of all females, and some male actors too. Chris is helping us all, from above. We are from the same source creator.

The soul of Christopher Reeve, and every other human, exists in the Higher Realm, where it is protected. The energy of the soul is the spirit. It is here in this temporary reality, trying to return to the soul to be one again. Its way is blocked by the dark energy that is taught by the invaders and their descendants. Understanding this is vital. It is a matter of either living or merely existing. Without this realization of Truth, the soul's spirit will continue to be enslaved. It will reincarnate as many times as necessary, until the spirit has been successful in discovering the reality of total freedom and the Knowledge to ascend to the Highest Realm, and remain there.

Our spirit is as a mirror of our soul. It is child-like, going out to play and experience, and possibly losing its way home. The moment our life cycle ends, the soul's childlike spirit will have been corrupted in the current reality within this consciousness. This causes the Knowledge to be lost or hidden. All souls are waiting for each enlightened spirit to return to the source energy. To affect the necessary changes within us, we must begin thinking and planning by expanding your mind and heart. We must learn to achieve the highest power of being, which is love, forgiveness, and happiness.

Negative energy converts to positive energy as we create positive cells. Their vibration will result in improving the reality through thinking, acting and feeling wholesome thoughts of love, as one people. As a thought is conceived, it creates a cell in the body, which is reinforced by the mind and heart. That one cell will continue to multiply, succeeding to a stronger vibration, bringing forth the experience, again and again as one body of energy of love.

Many are determined to succeed by practicing a reality that will deliver the results of bliss. People are standing taller than ever before. It takes time to grow a garden, however, and continued focus is required or relapses into negative thoughts can occur. This indicates that there are more bad cells within the body than good cells.

Replacing these cells requires understanding how all things are connected. We must see how applying this science, with intention, will manifest the process even faster. Once the spirit has built up enough good cells, they begin to either convert or push out the bad ones through bodily fluids. This process purifies the immune system by converting and overpowering the bad cells, creating a whole new reality. We advance by leaning on the stronger ones which are fully awakened.

I know this science because a brilliant scientist named Bruce Lipton discovered these cells and how they multiply influencing their environment. From studying his research, I made my own discoveries, if Liptons discovery yielded such proof of reproduction, then this also applies to cells of thoughts, expanding through repetition. Lipton's knowledge of cells helped me to understand how the mind, energy, and body interact with each other and with the energy outside our bodies, which is the environment. This fact of science teaches that once understood, the body has the ability to exchanged all bad cells for good, "love" cells, then disease, fear, or limitation cannot exist. In an illuminated, harmonious reality, the immune system of the body is powerful, rejecting the bad cells even faster. The current environment and the system of reality created by man holds our enlightenment hostage. This demands that we band together and stand united. This will forever end the system of darkness, and the reality it has yielded.

I know that I have experienced enough of this reality of cheap tricks. As we all come closer to the Third Peril, the Dark Matrix continues to affect its devastating strategy. The recent school shootings with high powered weapons, suggests their desire for us to be at war with each other. Society is under a form of hypnosis, controlled for thousands of years by the invaders. When they acquired the Knowledge of the Egyptian civilization, their rule for multiple thousands of years was assured. The events of today mimic the events of the past, just in a more modern time. Situations are recreated to keep society shackled from achieving ascension before the next Peril. Those humans, alive and functioning today, who support this cause through corrupt governance, have no idea what they are doing regarding their future existence. This is a critical time in our consciousness. The veil is slowing being lifted. The system that has steered our reality has been weakened tremendously. They are going to extremes to save their system of reality. The higher realm is fully involved now. Much of society have joined the cause by their own Free Will. We desire to live out our life cycle in love and peace. We desire this for all cultures around the world! We have the power from within to draw from our source energy and bring the beautiful bliss back to our reality.

The human mind reacts to, and remembers, all previous life experiences. No distinction is made as to type, time, or whether the experience is positive or negative. Our cells contain energy captured in tissue. They have their own, unique vibration. Those vibrations represent our thoughts from the past, present, and the future. These patterns of vibrations produce the emotions from our heart. They act as a magnet, bringing to us the experiences of bliss and sadness. We must understand our natural, scientific, and all-encompassing relationship to love, as a real, essential thing. We must experience love fully, to understand its profound power. There is a very important reason why we must do this. It will be fully disclosed why, near the ending of this book.

In my first book, The Pyramid of Love and Gratitude and the Laws of the Universe, I wrote of my personal discovery of the importance of love. That book is the foundation for what you are now reading. Both books combined will guide your journey toward freedom and self-discovery. You will understand the purpose of the pyramid, why it was created, and its vital, physical location. You will witness how it assists the "Anointed One", his quest to serve the Higher Realm, and his helping humankind vanquish the dark reality of the invaders of long ago who are causing the problems.

When human beings reflect on their own experiences, at whatever time of their existence, those experiences either improve or worsen our state of being. What occurs around us, continuously impacts the cells in our bodies. If we ignore this fact of science, we will be weakened inside.

When we understand how to connect to our cell's invisible energy, our Free Will allows us to stay connected, enabling our spirits to make choices. Our vibration and state of mind draw positive energy to us.

Throughout the history of civilization, and especially today, most human beings merely accept life as it comes. The overwhelming consensus believes that we are powerless to change anything on a grand scale. This belief is simple and easier to accept. The pursuit of Truth and Freedom, on the other hand, requires effort and the formulation of questions we need to have answered. Most people dislike questioning what is really going on because they may feel required to do something about it. In truth, no one single person can stop or alter the reality we all have been supporting for centuries. Together however, we can forever change this reality.

Our collective energies have great power. Our joined minds, sending out positive intentions, become one force of energy to eliminate the darkness, ignorance, hatred, pain and suffering that plagues the planet. We have no true option. We must do this for our loved ones, both here and above.

Once our energies align and the reality of the Knowledge of the superior realms is known, the encrypted cells within us will break free from the hidden exile. As the freedom continues to prosper, The Anointed One's purpose of so long ago will be finally realized. More superior Knowledge will come to us all. The cells will gradually reproduce at a much faster rate, which will be felt throughout the mind and the emotions. When this is achieved, our Soul's Knowledge will be attained. That awareness is the highest wealth we can achieve. It comes from the highest power of who we are, our source creator. It resides in the unseen, invisible energy that reacts to all of consciousness, just waiting to be called upon at any given moment. How magnificent that day will be!

## REVEALED KNOWLEDGE

- ▲ The cells are responsible for what we learn and know.
- ▲ Society is too busy learning and reacting to man's system, while neglecting what really matters the most.
- ▲ The cells make up who we are through previous life cycles, how we think, and what becomes of us.
- ▲ The key is creating a reality of love, and togetherness as one people.
- ▲ Wealth-creation cells emit a strong fear of losing all in this reality. Holding onto material possessions requires undermining others to remain in such a status.
- ▲ Material things are to be experienced only. To hold the mindset of ownership of things is a false concept by preventing us from discovering our higher selves.
- ▲ The cells know exactly when the life cycle will end. They are the past, present and the future.
- ▲ Alter your cells to experience, but also seek to reason deeper than on just a status level. This improves and strengthens the spirit to return to the soul in a whole form with the Laws and Knowledge led by the emotion of love, not greed.

# NOTES

# NOTES

# 5

# THE POWERFUL VORTEX OF THE MIND AND ITS SOUL

Applying Free Will enables the mind to think and create, by the vibrations of our desires. Our emotions are closely connected to all we do and experience. Like our cells, the mind has its own hidden secrets that are unknown to the human vessel. The action required to comprehend the vortex of the mind allows it to connect to the vast reaches of the Universe, where the highest realms of our existence reside. This is how the soul's spirit travels safely, through a beautiful vortex. A nanosecond of astral travel can equal light years of travel in the physical world. During astral traveling, a thin, silvery, antenna-like filament, joins your spirit and your Soul, allowing all spirits to travel and return safely through all physical matter.

During our normal waking state, our spirit exists almost in a lifeless state. It is permitted to come alive only when our individual ego and personality have entered a resting state, along with the body. During our sleep, the soul's energy awakens and can be freed from the bonds of our dark reality.

The mind and the spirit are responsible for all we see around us. Our cells record experiences of sight, sound and physical actions. To learn Alchemy is to learn the true purpose for our existence. It is the Science of how Free Will, the Mind, and the Soul come together as one. Once that is achieved, our world will no longer exist under the dark reality responsible for the chaos of war, fear, enslavement, oppression, and so much more. The deceivers know their time is short. They fear the awakening of us all.

Why must we bear witness to what we do? Our actions mold our realities. There is always a reason for all things. Something great is happening! Society has awakened from the false reality. It is past time to bring a purifying light to those causing the chaos. Those who resist our enlightenment must be exposed. The purveyors of the tools of war, allowing civilian children to murder savagely must be found out. The land barons and governments killing to control parcels of the Earth's surface must be defeated. The great religious institutions must be purged of the dark forces of control and power. Their true purposes must be learned and exposed.

Our innate ability to think in a clear, unfettered, state of mind, will lead to the truth. We are on track to discovery! We now understand who we are, and how we choose to exist. Like Dorothy from Kansas, we have had the choice all the time. Finally, we know why the expression of love is our greatest gift. We must love and forgive! In doing so, we dismantle the ultimate power of the darkness, forever.

The energy from our thoughts, sent via the mind and the emotions of the heart, pulls the elements together from the invisible realm of energy: atoms, carbon, cells, protons and molecules that comprise all things, including the human vessel. This is pure Science. Every human is reunited with source energy of love when we ascend to our origin between lives, and then we are sent back, unless we have already mastered the superior law, while in this powerful reality of consciousness.

Learning how to use science, to understand how our minds are responsible for everything we experience, is the most important understanding we could ever gain for ourselves, and for those around us, too. The true meaning of the Holy Grail is not a goblet. It is found in the energy of our DNA under a consciousness of "The Anointed One" This lives in each spirit, under an encrypted code, referred to as the Holy Grail. It represents the only reality we are to exist in. It is Love, found only in our DNA, not in the material world around us.

## REVEALED KNOWLEDGE

▲ The vortex of the mind allows all experiences to be born via the Free Will.
▲ Choices are a huge part of our experiences, both the good and bad.
▲ The mistakes we all make can leave scars of guilt. Let the mistakes go. They only serve as life lessons.

- ▲ Free Will means we can make a choice. We can go in either direction.
- ▲ Embrace your own powers within free will. Exist in a beautiful reality!

# NOTES

# 6

# THE THREE ELEMENTS OF ENLIGHTENMENT

Science is comprised of three elements. They are Energy, Matter, and Knowledge. They exist and are molded from our creative minds. The soul and the spirit are the invisible energy that engages the mind to think and create. If understood, and used properly, a beautiful reality will surface as a result from this practice.

Vibrational energy plays an important role in the creation process. A vibration of power and love, causes the Universe to react to those emitting that vital emotion, allowing us to envision and manifest the exact creation of our desires. By manifesting our desires in the present, we create the power of Knowing by experience. If we visualize it occurring in the future, then it will be delivered in the future. If we see it in the present moment, as real and already here, then it will appear almost in an instant.

Humankind relies on the concepts and illusions of the material world, where fear can overcome good judgement. Our ability to use our Free Will, in conjunction with the creative part of the brain/mind, has been cast aside, and replaced by a reality that has enslaved the living spirits of our world. Debt, in support of commerce, is enslavement to the true reality we are to exist in while we are here.

The material things that have been made will always remain, whether invented, naturally occurring, or purchased. These objects of matter exist as an example of what a creative mind or minds have brought into existence, by thinking and sending out a desire, along with the vision of having it in the physical form.

Creative vibration surrounds us. Simply consider what the minds of many, including our own, have created. As the mind thinks and emits that signal of creation, it continues to create. When we think and act upon someone else's instructions and programs we are not only limited, but also creating in an unreal reality. We are being led away from the influence of the anointed one.

Most prior creations of what we experience as our material world have been held in the powerful minds of the rulers of society. These selfish creations persist until they are purposefully dismantled. That necessary change must start with each of us. The only way to ensure a dismantling is through improvement to ourselves. Those individual acts of self-awareness will alter the collective consciousness for good in ways we can only imagine.

We will understand how governments repress the natural yearnings of the governed. Our skin color, language, or place of origin will hold no bearing on our love for each other. We will realize that we have limitless power. We will love people more, and the trappings of material influences less. We will re-dedicate ourselves to our love for our blue orb spinning in space where we all live. We will remain grateful for the blessings from planet Earth.

We must see our love to each other with fresh eyes. We will completely understand that I am you, and that you are me, and that together we are as one. We are powerful loving beings, unseparated by any provincial, parochial bias. We are all here to improve our reality, while saving our own consciousness.

We can be guided to these understandings if we simply reflect on the history and lives of the greatest culture, and the plight they overcame. The African people have journeyed long and hard to finally claim freedom. Their experience is our roadmap to fulfilling our destinies as well. They shared a focused, common purpose and desire and accomplished exactly what they desired! To be successful in our intentions, we must adopt the methods and strategies of the powerful Africans. Now, more than ever before, I am convinced the story of life continues to unfold.

While watching a recent documentary of Jackie Robinson I had a revelatory moment!It was as if a light bulb brightly illuminated my mind. I realized in that instant, that many, like the great baseball star, sacrificed themselves to pave the way for future generations. We must copy the methods of the Africans to return to our state of freedom in mind, body and spirit. There can never be a better culture to emulate to guide us back to the light. In my first book I suggested that the black man will lead us to salvation. I had no idea of how it would happen, only that it would. They are our mentors of Love and Gratitude and our shepherds through the dark.

We must realize that all things are completely created by someone's mind. We must recognize that we are taught to discriminate against other cultures. We must understand that we are born in this world to love, yet man will eventually require us to hate. The truth is there, simply waiting for us to uncover it.

If a mind is weak and pliable, it can be taught all the ways of the darkness. Until we change, and seek the true Knowledge, while discarding fear and self-limitation, we will not become free. The African culture understands this and are striving to live exceptional lives. We must seek their leadership in this most important struggle. I beseech them to lead us back to our Anointed Father, who reigns over our consciousness. Together, all peoples can return to their original state of power within superior knowledge, as we had in the very beginning of all things.

Why are there doubters of this path? It is because they have yet to comprehend the power that is within them. Our cells and DNA retain recordings and memories of every incarnation we have ever had, and, just as the skin cells reproduce, so do all cells in our body, recording every experience that ever occurred to us in this realm, in every life. Trust yourself. Look inside your heart. See who you really are.

Since your birth, controls have been placed on your reality. Your own energy has been channeled against us to keep us feeling limitation and fear, and to maintain our enslavement to the dark reality. We have been trained to focus on things that have no real value to our pursuit of enlightenment. The cells imprinted by man's system keeps us held down by our own limited Knowledge.

We do have the capability to tap into the superior Knowledge of understanding what is within us, to improve our lives. To do this, you must clear your mind and learn to focus on the inner sounds of peace, which the body emits through vibrations of sacred love, when you are in a deep, contemplative state and in harmony with nature around you. Once you have reached a state of enlightenment, you will begin to realize and understand the power of the mind. This will also provoke the encrypted cells to awaken the "Anointed One" that resides in you. His presence within your cells, will start the process of dissolving all the man-created experiences from your cell base of his Knowledge. As these cells are brought to the surface of reality, they vaporize the nonsense that has existed in and around us in the present consciousness.

## REVEALED KNOWLEDGE

▲ The Three Elements of Enlightenment are Energy, Mind, and Matter.

▲ We must understand the mind first to utilize the other two elements.

▲ How our vibration exists determines how we can create and improve our reality.

▲ People are often limited through the mind's thoughts. For example, many will not expand their own mind beyond what the system dictates. Governments purposely limit the reality of society to maintain control of the consciousness. Today a great shift in awareness is going on and the system will never be as it once was. The programming has been going on for multiple lives consisting of thousands of years. Layer upon layer of incorrect information and from generation to generation.

▲ To understand the two parts of Alchemy: one can be seen and created, whereas all creations (including human beings), harbor energy to be sustained.

# 7

# TO EXIST IN THE HIGHEST REALM OF ALL REALITIES

The reality of love is expressed in our energy via vibration. The vibration is unique and separated from the material reality. However, it remains connected to it through our love of our home planet and the elements she provides. The world of energy is always superior and stronger than the material world. It permeates things. What we do and what we have in the material world is never worth more than our consciousness. Our seed sprang from the most powerful realm of reality and creation. What we experience in all our frail humanity is self-created, even if we are applying our energies to actions created and bestowed upon us by others.

We must not allow ourselves to be trapped, earth-bound, when our cycle ends. We must pave our returning path to the Higher Realm with complete love and superior Knowledge. We must bring along the science of superior wealth derived from our powerful, enlightened mind.

I know that I was invited and encouraged by the "Anointed One" to return here. I understand fully the inherent risk. The controlling descendants of the ancient invaders are constantly creating chaos. Turmoil, misery, and darkness solidify their control over the reality. We were invaded eons ago, and reprogrammed to exist under this cloud of ignorance, fear, doubt, and limitation.

Prior to my most recent life cycles, in my past lives, I became influenced and confused. I lost my way. It has taken many cycles of life to regain my perspective and to reach this point. If my message remains unheard, I will be required to return to face an uncertain tomorrow. I will have to relearn everything and overcome more false realities of their agenda. My very reason for existence at this time in this place, is to simply ask everyone to seek their higher self. Read my words. Listen to your heart.

There is nothing in our lives that is superior to the Knowledge and purpose of the "Anointed One". Each of us must find their way and discover Jesus of Nazareth. Just look around and see what is in the correct flow of energy, then witness what and who are the limiting factors in your reality. See with open eyes, then think about what it all means. When one knows the Knowledge of love, through great experience, it is not difficult at all.

The Knowledge was shown to me through what I thought were dreams. Later, I would discover that I was seeing memories of what my spirit had witnessed and remembered from past life cycles. My ability to astral project out of my body has allowed me to connect to past experiences and prepare for future ones. My ability to write such knowledge is the proof of my convictions.

My Knowledge is not found in any man's textbook. Each person's soul has a library of laws created by our source and reside near the "Anointed One". Each person may visit this library, while they are living out their cycle of life in this realm. This is accomplished as the mind strengthens and the reality improves. If the mind remains unenlightened, the library will remain hidden and unknown. You have most likely visited your soul's library, but just can't remember, as the cells imprinted by the invaders of man create a thick, dense cloud preventing a waking reality to occur while erasing any Knowledge obtained while visiting the internal library of law.

In our current material world, the wealth that is created is not the wealth of the Higher Realm. Where it comes from and how it is obtained is most important. The buying and selling of land and structures are not creations of the mind, but of false reality of ownership created by man, influenced by the dark reality. No one can make claims on elements they did not create. All forms of commerce that include banking, money, and stocks are created to support the invading designers of the system, and those who serve them.

Whatever accumulation of these treasures we amass during our lives, will not influence our attempt to return to our soul when our cycle ends. We will discover that their pursuit, while alive, was merely a tremendous waste of our time and energies. Moreover, we will learn that we must return (reincarnate), and search for the blueprint of our source energy or forfeit our consciousness to serve them for eternity. We will fully understand that true wealth only comes about through the energy and Knowledge of the mind, and how the mind can process and connect to the invisible side.

Wealth only comes from the science of creativity of the mind. It is expressed through invention, music, visual art, performance art, and writing. All are connected to the energy of helping other people or helping our planet. Creating wealth must not perpetuate the concept of enslavement on anyone else. Every human possesses the ability to expand the mind and co-create whatever his or her soul desires, when existing in the correct reality.

Here's a short list of some of my favorite acting and musical performances. Their common thread is a powerful message to our hearts and minds. Their creation is a wealth of inspiration to us all. They include movies; It's a Wonderful Life, with Jimmy Stewart, and The Imaginarium of Doctor Parnassus, with Heath Ledger. Though there are many, a few songs that stand out are Chris Rea's The Road to Hell, John Lennon's Imagine and Mind Games, Earth Wind & Fire's Fantasy, and Todd Rundgren's Love is the Answer. The message in the lyrics reflect on "The Anointed One". A song that sends chills down my spine as tears run down my face is Get Together sung by Jesse Colin Young and the Youngbloods. Just pay close attention and hear the words. It will move your heart.

## REVEALED KNOWLEDGE

- ▲ Reality of the existence of energy is connected to the realm in which we all originated before we took physical form.
- ▲ When the cycle of anything ends, including plants, trees, and animals, the energy returns to the Source.
- ▲ Because of our consciousness, we can create both bad and good.
- ▲ All things require energy to exist and survive; even concepts require energy.
- ▲ It is a grand event to exist in peace and love.
- ▲ The meaning of wealth confuses most people. There is only one wealth: Love. To know and experience this type of wealth is our greatest purpose.
- ▲ Financial wealth will never compare to wealth of who we are and what resides in the depths of our energy.

▲ The poorest among us have nothing to lose and everything to gain. As enlightenment continues and the system of man crumbles, the poor and meek do not contend with the obsession of wealth. Instead, they find something worth far more in value, which is Love and Knowledge.

▲ The only wealth is Love.

▲ The Higher Realm is Love. Breath, think, and Love.

# 8

# THE REALITY OF WAR AND INHERITANCE: THE DARK TRUTH

The reality of war represents the untruth that by murdering others, one can create freedom. It only encourages ignorance and separation from our purpose. It creates trauma for people's spirits, which further enslaves them. It creates fear and limitation. It enforces a reality of enslavement. War creates an economic boom for the manufacturers of instruments of slaughter.

The economics of greed are used to rationalize reasons why we must have wars. These are the ideas of the dark matrix projected onto us. Be suspect of all justifications for conflict. Accept the truth that you might be the recipient of such conflict, designed by the invaders of man either in this life or a future one, thanks to the Law of Karma.

How does the Law of Karma work? When we send out energy, whether for bad or good, it surely will return to us, in either darkness or bliss. We cannot escape this part of consciousness. Our reality depends mainly on understanding how energy is produced by our own intentions driven by thoughts or ideas. This includes the vibrations of revenge or envy.

Often, we react when something has been done to us as individuals or to our country. Many believe in the old adage, "an eye for an eye." Of course, this kind of thinking never corrects a wrong, and, in fact, will only bring about more conflict. The purveyors of the dark reality invent situations, using the news media to spread the false narratives. This stirs up emotions in many to support an aggressive action. The invaders are expert liars. They are shameless. They allow actions to occur that bring loss of life. Their cold tactics are used to bring conflict to other parts of the world. If a leader refuses to follow this template, the invaders may create havoc by blaming on the country they are seeking to bully. I believe that the events of 9/11 2001 are a prime example of this deception.

The government of Saudi Arabia clandestinely assisted the United States in bringing this series of events to unfold. Controlling oil production was not a cause. Neither was imperial, US Middle eastern policies. The real agenda for the attacks is to dismantleJesus Christ from Western Culture primacy in the distant future, in order to make way for their New World Order. The attacks by US forces in Iraq served the purpose to blend the reality of those from that region, who are taught to denounce Christ as our savior of consciousness. This obvious reasons, to begin relocating Middle Eastern refugees to America. This plan, well thought out, has set in motion the elimination of Judaism, Catholic and Christianity.

Although the coming Third Peril is unavoidable. We cannot prevent it or affect it. We can prevent the dark reality from control of our lives after the expansion of Earth. We can even dismantle their control over us and change the course of their sinister world plans. If we, one-by-one, learn to follow the "Anointed One's" knowledge. If we truly love all. If we do not judge others, regardless of what has been done. If we forgive those who trespass our purpose. Our ability to love each other unconditionally is our greatest act to perform.

By adhering to those life tenets, we will allow the mind to understand the Science that I have explained in this book. We must not allow any singular culture to force their reality on us. Only by joining together as one can we prevail. If one's beliefs harbor any darkness, that world view cannot be tolerated as we enlighten ourselves to humankind's freedom. We must rise up mentally, by creating and practicing a pure reality based on love.

War achieves only one goal. It succeeds at creating a diversion in order to separate people. It keeps our minds busy with dealing with endless crises. In so doing, we are prevented from connecting to the superior law of the Master's Knowledge of the "Anointed One". The mind must be relentlessly burdened and constantly broken, to prevent it from acknowledging its ability to seek the freedom of the spirit on the astral plane. War leads our young, healthy spirits into the delusion that it is honorable to die for a freedom that really does not exist. Countries near conflict exude a sense of nationalism. Flags, bunting, and ceremony stir the citizen's patriotic fervor. The insane notion is created that making the supreme sacrifice is somehow worthy of a warrior of freedom. This is tragically false! Do not encourage your child to forsake their true selves for a reality not supported by the "Anointed One".

Any spirit who dies in war will have the horrors of war as their last experience recorded into their cells in this powerful consciousness of the "Anointed One". That will be where their next cycle will be served, unless the mother relocates to another area, and, even then, that spirit will find its way back to the last experience of where his or her physical bodies died. Spirits are drawn to repeat the same experience again if the Knowledge is not discovered in this reality.

Seeing things clearly may help the young understand that being born means to live and love. They can realize that they were born of a higher source of energy of both male and female that reflects in us all. Energy is intended to live and record everything, down to the smallest detail, Because of the shock, horrors, and trauma of war, the spirit never realizes the truth of life's purpose. Real freedom is the reality to love everyone!

We all have a real opportunity to live out our purpose, knowing what is real, you and me. Our mind can open and be in a reality of freedom. No person of this Earth can give me freedom. It is not theirs to give. I am already free. The light of freedom shines brightly for all. The first day I could see the light was pure bliss, completely overwhelming.

# REVEALED KNOWLEDGE

- ▲ We've been taught that war is necessary for freedom, but war is quite the opposite of freedom.
- ▲ War is a tool to entice compliance that there is a wager to remain free. This is a huge lie. There is only one freedom and it isn't connected to this realm of existence.
- ▲ In the Pyramids of Giza, the fourth side represents the Iron Age. The Pyramids line up exactly to three stars (Suns) within Orion, and our home exists within Orion's belt. Why not a three-sided Pyramid? Four sides depict the separation of the two realms.
- ▲ The Three sisters of the feminine womb of the anointed one, that is Christ, represents are the three suns. We are from that galaxy, where our anointed Messiah is from. Through many minds, He is finally expelling the aliens of man from his throne!

▲ The next time you look at Orion's belt, know your soul exists there in a highly secured state; it is your spirit here that is trapped and must be set free by the truth. Love is our greatest achievement, the highest wealth we will ever own. As the cells convert, the vibration reaches the heavens of Orion's belt, where the anointed one resides.

▲ Do not encourage your children to become politicians or war subjects. We birth them for a greater purpose for the Higher Realm – NOT for the benefit of the aliens within the governments, elites, or religions.

▲ No government or any member of society will ever own this planet. Do not be tricked into fighting for something that is not yours or mine. We all are here for a specific amount of time. What we learn and obtain is measured when our cycle ends. War is nothing but a dirty trick to guarantee each soldier will return to serve the alien force. Men of the anointed one, must wake up now. Do not serve the alien force again in a repeated life in another cycle.

# 9

# THE CONSCIOUSNESS OF THE ANOINTED ONE: THE MOST SUPERIOR PART OF OUR EXISTENCE

Since we were children, we have heard parents and preachers describe the "soul". What they always assumed was that it was wholly part of our living body. It is not. Your soul and my soul, the part that is pure energy, actually resides in the unseen world of spirit, in the system of Orion, where the Christ consciousness exists. We are forever connected to The Christ Consciousness.

The Knowledge is encrypted in all spirits. It connects two distinct realities; an inner one of higher self, and an outer, physical one, of this reality, which originated from our source creator. The soul is the oracle to our encrypted Knowledge, providing a blueprint to our spirit. Only after we discover the proper Knowledge in our current consciousness, by our spirit's connection to the soul and its library, will the spirit return and remain in the Higher Realm. Only then will the soul be whole and complete, fully protected.

The powerful, feminine energy must rise to her birth purpose and save our male counterparts from themselves, by assisting to return them into their original role and reality. We must save mankind from continuing to be lost and displaced. The feminine energy will continue to express knowledge, gratitude and love, striving to bring world peace through these acts. All spirits, vibrating with feminine energy, will rise above the dark system designed to limit our gender and enslave man. All females must return to their powerful beginnings, recalling the time of Lilith, who refused to lie beneath man. Her powerful mind created life within her womb by mere thought. That amazing ability to create life by thought is how the Higher Realm produces life through the power of feminine energy. The "Anointed One" is proof of this truth, created by thought in an unspoiled virgin.

There are symbols we must see and recognize for what they truly represent. Inside our universe is a symbol of a triangle. It represents the Alchemy in our physical temple (our body). In each of us is our inner, three-dimensional, Pyramid of Knowledge. It symbolizes our Wealth of Soul and our capacity of Love. It acts to neutralize and balance the current reality of suffering and enslavement. This exists through Christ consciousness. Within his eternal wisdom there is a place for us all. We are fueled by his energy to decode this reality through his symbol in numerology. That is the number three. The holy trinity resides within all of us. The Pyramid of the "Anointed One", is the symbol connecting us to our celestial home, far away, within the three stars of the constellation Orion, located in the Cosmos, in the wondrous, nightly sky.

The mind must be prepared and ready to rise above the forced deception. It is imperative that we accept responsibility for all that is created in our reality. At the beginning of this life, all spirits are born in a body of matter, existing in a free state of reality. The physical shell for our spirit "lives" a temporary experience in this realm of reality. At death, the spirit and its shell return to our origins in the Cosmos, hopefully having achieved The Knowledge, to remain spiritually whole. It is important to understand that to obtain a shell for our energy, we must be born into a body of matter in this plane.

The second purpose for our existence is to experience matter; being matter, being surrounded by matter, and creating objects from matter. Upon ascending to the Cosmos after our cycle is complete, we then return to our beautiful, loving soul. All our discoveries and achievements are recorded and stored in our endless database of "cells".

We all must take our place in this reality, own up to our responsibility as powerful humans, and prepare to finally break free from the reality we all have been existing under. We must prepare to go home to our souls.

Our first steps to this eventual, eternal bliss is relinquishing the dark reality forced on us by the alien creators. We all must be teacher and student, diligent in working together to see the validity of what is being presented. My soul's purpose is to enlighten every willing person who walks the face of this Earth. We cannot be deterred by doubters. We must create a reality based on truth and purpose. The day will come when what has been written becomes evident. The time draws nigh. Listen with your heart.

Remember the purpose for the life and death of Jesus of Nazareth. He came to guide our spirits. His aim was to teach us wisdom, through love and kindness. He wants us all to reopen our mind's eye (the third eye), and our hearts, to see that we were derailed from the blueprint of our soul by a false reality, created by an alien race, a very long time ago, that was imposed on humankind when the aliens first rewrote the Knowledge, banning our birth right.

We must improve our reality to return to our blueprint. Remember...we are love, we are power, and most of all, we can be whole with the "Anointed One"!

As your spirit grasps the message of my book, it will prompt you to act. A sort of synchronistic event will occur. People of your new reality will appear out of nowhere. Thoughts and ideas will be shared. This will create a beautiful vibration of love. We support each other in our new enlightened state of reality.

Tackle the little things that are easily identified as dragging down your reality. As you deal with the small ones, the reality continues improving and shifting you toward a fresh, new direction, felt in the heart. It will push the mind to desire to improve even more. This is how the false, alien reality can be vanquished from your life. I believe we are approaching the ending point of the darkness.

There is much to learn in the decoding of the current, false reality. Together, with all working side by side, we are embarking on a new journey into the light of self-discovery. We must understand why the current reality has limited us all. The controllers must be identified. We must not lose the truth. The key to recapturing the True Reality has been among us all along. The "Anointed One" existed and ascended from it, to complete our source of creation's work from the Higher Realm. Many spirits assisted him in his divine purpose. Christ's mission was to free every spirit, forever. The time has come to understand and accept that truth, before the Third Peril.

He sacrificed his existence in the other reality, came here, into this reality, and then returned to the higher reality. He helped those who volunteered, over time, to come to this world and dimension to continue to free us from the enslavement we have known for way too long here on Earth.

There are two distinct cultures of society that are aware of what is about to happen to the planet. When Earth self-destructs, our reality, within our consciousness, will be at great risk. The planet is expanding, as it has twice before. The event that enabled the Jews to flee Egypt, retold Biblically as the Exodus was, in actuality, the Second Peril.

The Third Peril will be worse than the other two. The physical part of our existence will see great devastation. We must improve our reality to save our consciousness. Earth will reclaim much of her assets of elements in order to grow and expand.

The individuals who created the reality we are releasing, have been working hard to remove history in preparation for this cataclysmic event. The two cultures who shared The Knowledge through the Second Peril are fighting for the next rule of reality in this consciousness. Dismantling history in America is to dismantle the "Anointed One". That is the real agenda. To eliminate him from this reality. By doing so, they create an existence that sanctions our consciousness to exist in total darkness. These two cultures exist in a fool's reality. This planet will not harbor life again for a very long time to come.

Regardless, unless these two cultures stop fighting and stop waging wars, they will become lost as those of the last peril. There will be mass loss of life. It can't be avoided. If the world does not heed this warning and take the necessary actions to improve its reality, prior to this event, a New World Order will control, in a lost dimension.

Their reality, absolutely creates hatred among us all. The two cultures responsible for the darkness are the Jews and Islam. Both started from the "umbrella" of Abraham. Together, they created constant chaos involving other countries and continents. Their fighting continues to separate us from returning to who we once were. The last Peril of this planet and her previous expansion led to our enslavement.

History has retold the story that God instructed Moses to lead his people out of Egypt to escape bondage. This wasn't a directive from God or any other entity. This was energy expanding. The Red Sea descended due to the second peril, allowing Moses to lead as many to safety as possible. Their forty years of wandering in the desert were not because they were lost. It was time needed to reprogram their reality that originated from their previous existence. Recreating a new reality meant exposure to unlimited knowledge. New cells were created, improving their reality of enslavement.

This is how they rebuilt their reality that has survived for nearly 4,000 years. Moses was true to the higher realm. His purpose, however, was not honored and carried out by his followers. There is nothing more important than for all of humanity to evaluate the past and recognize all, including Christ, who sent out a loud and clear message to "wake up" and realize we are so much more than what we have been programmed to believe.

We must grasp The Knowledge and Truth and embrace it, as if we would embrace the love of our life. We must practice this Knowledge and allow the spirit to live again in unlimited reality, by the powers of our own encrypted blueprint that our source created for us all. The spirit is never permitted to return to its soul, unless the true Knowledge has been rediscovered in this reality, and carried back to the soul, mirroring the soul's Knowledge.

We must strengthen as many spirits as we possibly can. The destruction for Earth is not man's doing. It will occur in the very near future. Events will unfold and there is nothing anyone can do to stop it. Our only action is to learn what is required of us. We are tasked with strengthening the spirit and returning to our natural origins where we will be whole, once again.

This Higher Realm of reality is just waiting to be summoned into existence by each spirit to balance the paradigms once and for all. We hold the key to a freedom that only our source has created. We are here on borrowed time (because time is running out). We must free our spirits by learning the science and the purpose of Love and Gratitude before we return to Christ.

I am only one of many individuals, who have been awakened to work through the anointed one's guidance and superior Knowledge. He allowed me to learn from countless, trying situations. I was tested on many levels, pushing forward to the next platform of knowing. The lessons never end as I stay committed to his purpose

## REVEALED KNOWLEDGE

- ▲ Most are unaware of the truth about who Christ is and his connection to all who share in this consciousness.
- ▲ Earlier in my life, I didn't follow or believe in Christ; I saw him only as a wise prophet and questioned the concept of a "virgin birth."
- ▲ I have not read the Bible, the Torah. Or the Koran. I will not. My cells possess Knowledge from long ago. It does not serve my purpose to co-mingle my knowledge with words written by the man.
- ▲ People must raise their consciousness by loving more, forgiving all for their mistakes, and avoiding judgement of others.

▲ Grasping the power of saving our consciousness, by improving our reality, yields amazing rewards.

▲ Remember, the cells in the body are what the Higher Realm reads

▲ We must rise above our mistakes and forgive ourselves. No burden should ever be carried to the other realm.

▲ We live and exist in the most powerful realm, but we have been limited in our ability to comprehend the powers we have within.

▲ The system of man has deliberately smothered our birth codes to keep our spirits captive for their reality, purpose and agenda.

▲ The elements of this planet are intended for everyone to learn and experience – not for an alien force to create a system of limits and sanctions based on race, status or location.

▲ We have great Knowledge to expand our minds together

# NOTES

# NOTES

# 10

# OUR VIBRATION SUSTAINS OUR REALITY

Our reality connects to our energy and is influenced by our actions. When we learn to control our emotions, and use our minds in a positive way to envision the outcomes we truly desire, we conquer this reality and bring about the rebirth of our essence, one soul at a time, in unity. We then acquire the newly created, self-perceived reality, born out of the spirit of the love and unity that we have achieved together with our hearts and minds. The Universe and its laws react to the strongest minds that have mastered how to use the Knowledge, rendering the desired or undesired outcome.

What will the new reality of this world be like? So many changes will occur. Future attorneys will not be practicing the laws of the alien race, but rather the laws of source Knowledge. This is the superior law of science, energy, and love, with the guidance of the "Anointed One", Christ. The New World Order will be an order of truth. The natural laws will be practiced and honored for eternity. The two realms will become one once again. Earth will finally be a planet of peace and enlightenment.

The designed laws of the alien race will shift from their current design and return to the natural laws that previously governed our wonderful planet and universe. As I described earlier, that is the feminine energy of love and unity, creating life out of love and bliss. The future of this planet rests squarely in the hands of every female alive in this consciousness. We will re-assume our original place as the offspring of our feminine creator.

I am a strong, thriving female. I am spiritually attuned to the light. I am imprinted with love, not darkness. My vision is for everyone to capture the magic and power of their own capable minds, and expand their experience, without the reality of fear or the false paradigms that have held us all down.

Love is the key source of the life fulfillment we have sought all our entire lives. That is not a truism born from any sort of religious dogma. Organized religion has failed humankind, denying the Knowledge of the mind and of Alchemy to every living spirit. The world's religions were created and maintained by the male ego. The true purpose of the feminine energy has been expunged from any teaching.

An early example occurred in the late fourteenth century. Nicolaus Copernicus was retained by the Catholic Church in Rome to map the planets, and to scientifically prove that the Earth was located at the center of the universe. As you might recall from school, a problem arose for the astronomer. His calculations led him to the unequivocal conclusion that the Earth was, indeed, not at the center of the Universe. In fact, his research yielded the result that the Sun is the center of our Universe.

Copernicus presented his findings to the Church hierarchy. In turn, they demanded him to write an official summary exactly as they desired, with no deviation. Obviously, the Catholic Church of six hundred years ago cared little for the scientific truth. Their entire aim was to continue to control the masses through fear, lies, and misinformation.

In another instance, we can use the life's work of the great Italian mathematician, astronomer, philosopher and also a Cardinal of the Catholic Church, Galileo, as an example of how organized religion would silence and suppress scientific discovery to protect their interests. He did not deny that God, the creator, exists. He believed in God. But, other than what he observed in the ocean tides, he had no scientific proof of the Earth's movement. Still, he thought there was more to learn. This led him to investigate the Copernican heliocentric theory (Earth and planet revolve around the sun), confirming as true after inventing the most powerful telescope at that time and by taking many years to log careful observations.

The Roman Inquisition of 1615 proclaimed him guilty of promoting heresy. The Catholic Church ordered his imprisonment. For the last twelve years of his life, he remained a prisoner in his own home, preventing him from sharing his Knowledge and insight with the world. But, since Truth cannot be held down, word did get out, which is why we know his story.

Why would the Church persecute such a man? A cardinal, even? Could it be that the Church knew the truth, and needed to hide the fact that their own conceptions or interpretations of the stories of creation were grossly wrong?

The Catholic Church of the sixteenth century promoted the idea that man was the center of the universe. Since man was the most important creation of God, removing the Earth from the central position among the planets meant dislodging him from his lofty position in importance to the Creator. Therefore, the Church imprisoned the "heretics". The truth would remain hidden, they avowed, to control the reality of man both then and now. I believe that religious organizations are guilty of suppressing Knowledge. They are as culpable as the murderers throughout history, slaying millions of spirits to maintain their control of the reality of all minds in the physical realm by imprinting the experience of death onto the molecules located within the cells.

## REVEALED KNOWLEDGE

▲ Our vibration and reaction to outer situations reflect the condition of our inner cells.
▲ The cells were created to teach and instill a memory to help the operator do the job efficiently.
▲ Within our cells exists memories of multiple past lives. Each life cycle has been recorded in the server of the Universe.
▲ The Universe has an endless capacity to store our data. It also holds the encrypted Knowledge that only Free Will can activate. This Knowledge has occupied the mind for many thousands of years.
▲ Real Freedom and Love is the Knowledge stored in our cells, which we have had for eternity.
▲ Our reality creates our vibration and how we are programmed to think. It emits the vibration of our emotions. For some, man's system creates fear and doubt.

# 11

# THE HIGHEST PURPOSE OF CHRIST

The "Anointed One" was born to teach us to serve our source of creation, and the laws that govern this universe. He did not come to Earth to create religious institutions in his name that would serve to enslave the spirits he was crucified trying to save. The Bible and the holy writings of other world religions were intended to be used as guides for all humanity to evolve to a Higher Realm of understanding, and to prove to everyone the truth of our abilities.

Each person should be able to freely choose their own desires. By knowing the truth, the mind has the power to think and create by just a thought. Instead, the science that would have revealed our purpose was deliberately left out of the Bible. That was done specifically to preserve the practice of using God as a sort of meal ticket, allowing so-called, religious leaders to trade in the "business" of salvation for profit.

It doesn't matter how much a person donates to a church, synagogue or mosque if they do not discover and practice their purpose for existence. One may pay to enter any establishment one chooses in man's reality. However, no one shall pay a monetary fee to enter the Higher Realm. That is a birthright. Yet is must be earned in this reality through Science and Knowledge of the mind that creates and leads to a reality of love.

The corruption of basic, life truths and their true purposes compels my writing of this book. I understand, as should you, the existence of a dark network. Its function is to act as a sort of safety net for the corrupt few controlling our reality. The infection of our lives reached to religion, banking, and government. The average person accepts this reality and all the laws made by these hybrid invaders, who are not of this world or even this dimension. To insure complete fealty to their purpose, the dark controllers created the threat of suffering, whether death or pain or limitation. The result is acquiescence through fear. We have allowed our silent ignorance to sustain by giving away the light of love, Knowledge, and energy. Further, we have been unwilling (as humans collectively) to allow ourselves to suspect that some people may be so evil as to impose upon us a deceptive reality.

Regardless of what they do to us, we must not accept the actions of their intent. We must remain free of fear, hatred or judgment. This is how they have trapped us for thousands of years. If you are ever in a situation facing death by this alien race, close your eyes. You do not want to keep a vision of what is coming. Do not record their actions with your windows to your soul.

When we produce negative emotions such as greed, grief, anger, or revenge, vibrational signals are created. Our experiences from past lives through this current life are stored in our cells. These emotional vibrations can trigger us to repeat the same experiences as before in a past life cycle. These recordings are then delivered into the data storage system of our spirit, and upon ascension at the death of the body, the spirit enters a buffer, carrying our total experiences. Fortunately, our soul is shielded from the dark Knowledge of the alien controllers. Ourspirit returns to Earth to incarnate again, continuing to reuse the bad information from many past lives. Returning to the real Knowledge is a process, a cleansing of the spirit. When the enlightenment finally occurs, the soul is ready to accept the spirit for eternal bliss. As spirits awaken, the vibration is felt by others. We can see the contrast clearly. We know exactly what to do. This is the absolute best time to be alive!

Once the energy of us all finds the real Knowledge, the law library of each spirit will finally be discovered. We will realize that we had access to it the whole time. Now we can think critically. We know our intuition is real and not a figment of our imagination. Once we understand that all situations are created to provoke a reaction that sustains their agenda, we will behave to sustain our power, instead of giving it away.

The souls who knew Christ in the flesh, his Apostles and close disciples, were instructed to teach the power of the mind, the importance of Love and Gratitude, and how to be co-creators of the Universe with our source creator. Christ and his disciples ascended to a civilization in the Cosmos of our Universe. This is not the story of the Bible. It is the true accounting of the Higher Realm.

The truth of our existence should be shared freely, with dignity and wisdom. However, because of the oppression by religions and the suppression of truth, we now must search for it independently. Empowerment is the only purpose for us to exist in this consciousness. We must all be enlightened in the new world of a new order. Schools of enlightenment will replace the alien-created system of education. The reality of schools has taught children to be enslaved to concepts of debt, commerce, taxes, and the support of war. These subjects do not benefit any of us once the life cycle ends.

Our Founding Fathers, I believe, knew these alien invaders and complied with their demands. Their descendants are among us today. Recorded history describes the detail of man's blind belief in acquiring wealth. It would take more brilliant humans, born much later, to achieve the empowerment, seek out the truth, be certain of its validity, and teach the entire world the hidden truth that we are not from Earth, our soul is protected in another dimension, and only the spirit can experience other realities (and our dimension).

Once you achieve the understanding of how the mind should be used, along with its functions and capabilities, with the correct application of the laws of energy, you will begin to feel changes. Alchemy is the process we engage in daily. We contribute every day, whether we use our energy to co-create a greater reality of truth and pure love, or to sustain the current reality of fear and limitation. We do have a choice.

If we want to see Truth, all we need to do is ask, and it will be shown. The mind must be open to begin the process. Desire leads to results. Reading the correct information is the key to expanding the mind. Never speak the words, "I don't have time to learn or seek this Knowledge." That is part of the design of the alien force, to keep you enslaved from reaching your highest potential.

Once the world is supplied with pure Knowledge, the path to the Golden Age of Enlightenment will reappear. Every man, woman, and child will exist by his or her very own law of desire and love at the highest vibration of action and apply the science of creation, using their minds as the navigator. The reality of war will no longer be required in this world. The spirit will finally become "as one" with the soul again by rediscovering the original blueprint of Knowledge in this current consciousness and returning to the protected soul, proud and complete.

# REVEALED KNOWLEDGE

- ▲ Christ, The Messiah who embodied the greatest purpose of a man, was someone I did not believe in, until the year 2000 when I briefly crossed over.
- ▲ As my spirit rose above this planet, I discovered the greatest tragedy – the chaos of consciousness from my vantage point high above.
- ▲ My encounter with Christ, a man I doubted my entire life, was miraculous.
- ▲ Being an old soul and learning I was trapped in this realm filled me with anger. I shared my feelings that the Higher Realm had done little to help us down here.
- ▲ At first, I refused to return. I was kept in a beautiful room with great furnishings and lovely sage-green walls, but I was only permitted to reside there for three days – right down to the second I had exited.
- ▲ Before my return, I went before the Messiah and begged Him not to send me back, but to my surprise, he told me it was not under his control; Universal Laws dictated I go back to my earthly existence to serve a purpose no one else dared to take on.
- ▲ My cell base was at zero at that time; my Knowledge had been completely covered up by man's schemes and tricks. These events really did occur. My voice was heard loud and clear.
- ▲ The Government is working on Christ's behalf by eliminating all history. They want to remove all religions.
- ▲ Christ is our consciousness and he has already prevailed against the devil of darkness, which is man
- ▲ We are connected to Orion and the three suns. We must trust in Christ, not religion.
- ▲ We must understand our purpose is far greater than the system that has existed for many thousands of years.
- ▲ Christ will continue to weaken the system of man, religion, and government.

▲ Love is the key to destroying the system of control man has used to enslave the spirit of each human.

▲ Christ's highest purpose is to ensure his people prepare for the journey home, while we are alive in the present consciousness.

# NOTES

# NOTES

# 12

## ALCHEMY AND THE ENERGY OF THE MIND

The mysterious ways our brain can transform and transmute matter, and how it functions with the vortex, is the secret to understanding our true being. The "Alchemy" of the soul and mind complements the alchemy of material things. I know how the formula of Alchemy works. It is connected to the mind, driven by the passion of the heart. It works in tandem with the cause of all things, manifesting in our presence. Begin the process for yourself right now. Clear your mind. Allow yourself to meditate on space and time in a relaxed state of consciousness. Now, visualize the vortex of the mind. You are taking the first step.

When we walk in light, fulfilling our true purpose, a state of pure consciousness can serve to manifest the things we seek. What we conceive in our minds eventually crystallizes in our current reality. It is composed of atoms, molecules, cells, carbon, and energy. Our minds constantly create, in a conscious state or not. We create everything we draw to ourselves by the signals we emit. These vibrations eventually become the experience of our desired thoughts both good or bad.

There are two sides of Alchemy: the first is the concept of material matter. The other is the energy force that reacts from the command of the mind. The soul and its spirit are pure energy. They contain all the buried Knowledge that only Free Will can activate. The Universe, the soul, and the mind are symbiotic. They are mutually sustaining and exist as one. The cells, present in all things, are infused by the energy of thought, enabling us to co-create all that has been, and all that will be, in the past, present, and future. This powerful, life-changing Knowledge has been within us all since birth. To activate, only a few actions are required. Initially, one must apply our Free Will. This action will allow each mind to design and make choices that no other can suppress.

Consider your physical surroundings. Look carefully. View it all; the furniture, the art, your clothing, and that kitchen full of appliances. Realize that it has taken an unlimited number of minds to create these, many things. While we take a visual inventory, are we trying to understand how each piece came to be? No. We take it for granted.

More often than we realize, the people who create things have done so unaware of the Alchemy of how they have achieved it. Many create solely for wealth, seeking an earthly state of happiness. Accumulating riches can never give the heart what it needs to feel complete. Only the acquisition of the Knowledge through science and logic will bring to each spirit the true and lasting reality of the power of love.

When quantum physics is not understood, the material things we create can be co-opted by others. Understanding the mechanics of the creation of all things will eliminate their control and disarm their power. For example, if any organization created a reason to take anything from you, your Knowledge of the science of creation would enable you to reproduce the exact same thing – or something even better – the next time. Let them take it all, smile at them and shake their hand. By golly, thank them from the bottom of your heart! Keep your power and let the object go. They have transferred power to a material item that would not and could not exist unless a mind had created it; this is where we must comprehend that the practice of placing our power in objects, as taught to us by the alien force and their human helpers, limits our ability to experience Free Will.

The spirit of mind holds powers that come, not from Earth, but from a source connected to the spirit and soul. The body is connected to the elements of what Earth.. The spirit is the reflection of its own soul, providing all our powers and abilities. We are to only experiment within this reality and not become obsessed with any material creation.

Because we cannot really own the things of the Earth, what we create is never ours to keep. The world system has placed all energy into ownership of something. The fact remains that the substance it requires is only on loan to us. It was never meant to be ours for eternity. The ingredients required to create all material matter solely belong to this planet. We all must detach from the material creations of our desires. Failing to do so will put constraints on the spirit, preventing it from gaining the required Knowledge for the soul to be free.

The elements of our planet were provided to us for experimentation. We continue to learn, through our ability to create from a thought. We seek to be made aware of the invisible force of energy that vibrates outward toward creation, and reacts to a confident mind, once enough cells have built up in one's body, through manifesting, to create the desired reality. This energy was responsible for infusing together the elements that are required to bring forth our desires and thoughts. All experiences, both good and bad, are recorded. We came to Earth to experience "life" outside our perfect realm. This was to be the Alchemy of two worlds existing as one whole; one that could be seen, and the other existing in an invisible state of energy.

When the unseen, other world was cut off from our existence and reality, all who resided here became enslaved, due to the misuse of this power by a few, to control the mind and spirit. In my own research, the truth of this science has yielded to me the ability to draw from my own spirit. I have mastered the ability to travel back to my soul, where my library exists in the Higher Realm, to pull into this dense reality and deliver accurate Knowledge. There is nothing to fear and everything to gain by taking the necessary steps to inform your own spirit of the true Knowledge.

Each of our lives is brief. What we achieve or create in material form in this consciousness, is intended to lead us closer to the source truth. It will completely free our minds. Our life's purpose now is to carefully re-examine the Knowledge and find the path that will educate the spirit. The spirit must seek the Knowledge that mirrors its own soul, and upon the death of the body, the spirit will be permitted back into its soul because the correct blueprint will be present: LOVE.

We have earned the right to have and harness the superior Knowledge we expanded upon while in this powerful state of consciousness and take the earned Knowledge with us to the other side, when the physical vessel expires. Our body, made of all elements of matter and carbon, will also continue to reside in this realm of existence, as it too is only on temporary loan during our stay in this life. The spirit and soul become as one, finally going home for eternity, infused with love. This is my final reincarnation. I was asked to return to assist the "Anointed One", and to help mankind. I will return to the "Anointed One" with the required Knowledge. Under no circumstances do I plan to waver on my intention to not return and live through another lifecycle.

I know I have achieved what was required in several past lives to remain in that perfect realm. Because I mastered it so well, Christ encouraged me to return and expand my ability within the world. Now is the time to start building the cells of love and light. Many have fallen short of learning this Knowledge, only to find out the truth when their time arrives to ascend to the higher realm, love must be of the spirit or the destination of the spirit will be the buffer zone, before entering the Higher Realm for what will be only a brief visit. The buffer zone is created by our own limitation and fear, which the alien force created for those to remain in ignorance. The buffer zone also acts as a screen to prepare us for the shock of learning what our responsibility was while we lived here on Earth. There is never any judgment, as it is understood that we had limited Knowledge, and through it all our spirit had been nearly destroyed by this alien realm of reality. We must pay our dues upon returning to Earth in a new body. Whatever you experienced in a past life, while in this consciousness, will determine if the buffer zone is where you will go before entering the higher dimensions.

The reason the buffer zone is in place is to prevent any residual from this realm from contaminating the pure realm with what was experienced here, in the alien forces' dense reality of ignorance and limitation. This refers to what the cells recorded. It is related to the science of Karma and the way in which we design the future by our ability to love or be loved, our greatest achievement in this consciousness.

By learning the true Knowledge of what the soul requires, the spirit can bypass the buffer zone. This reality was once quite dense with concepts and illusions, until the anointed one instructed me to create his Pyramid. Once it had remained in this existence for seven years, the "Anointed One" could effortlessly penetrate the minds of all spirits, allowing mankind to gain the mental strength necessary to overcome the influences of the alien force.

It is astonishing to learn what we can achieve in the consciousness of our lives. Residing within us is the blueprint of the love and Knowledge. We are bestowed with the ability to create all we can imagined. Our greatest experience comes through helping others. The act of giving is immensely powerful for the spirit.

My only desire is for all to reach the same level of Knowledge as I. This will enable humankind to exist in a reality of love and bliss. The genie of our dreams is provided by our own soul. The beautiful soul is the force of our creation. It can deliver every desire we could imagine. We are truly demigods, living in a temporary state of consciousness.

All humans can master the Knowledge. Many however, dismiss conscious creation as too difficult to accomplish. I challenge you today, right now, to make a commitment to yourself to expand your mind by exercising critical thinking and realize that you have powers beyond your own comprehension. The current system, designed to create fear and helplessness, creates doubt in the minds of many. Yet, your mind can bring forth results projected by your cells.

The Knowledge belongs to the world. Every human has a library of their encrypted blueprint, recorded in their cells, consisting of past lives and all experiences. I am not unique. Everyone has the same blueprint, although our life experiences differ. Today I am fully aware of my purpose, what I know, and why I write as I do. I am here, in this place and time, to serve the anointed one and bring his message of Love, Gratitude, and Peace.

## REVEALED KNOWLEDGE

- ▲ The Alchemy of Energy is both seen and unseen.
- ▲ There are two characteristics of Alchemy: material matter that forms into what seems like a solid or can be seen, and the energy that resides in every material object.
- ▲ The human body is the most unique of all matter. Each human's energy remains protected in the physical vessel comprised of all elements of the Earth, including iron, water, and electricity. The energy within each human being is connected to another realm of existence.
- ▲ Alchemy is both invisible and visible. Previously, it was thought to be only chemistry, liquids, or alloy metals.
- ▲ If the world could grasp the science of how things function from energy, transforming from our current existence through Alchemy and Quantum Physics would be simple.
- ▲ The mind must expand to grasp the capabilities of the energy it requires to exist in a non-material environment.

# 13

# THE SOURCE OF OUR KNOWLEDGE

How intelligent we are, and how we learn, affects the entire universe. The planets in our solar system form an actual network that communicates with the Higher Realm. We must evolve constantly, infusing that Knowledge into our minds from our souls as a continual pattern of thought if we are to evolve in a harmoniously balanced manner. We must exit this reality equipped with what is required for our spirit to return to its own soul, with the heart beaming with love and Knowledge of experience that reflects the blueprint in the cells of our human body.

Our energy contains the Knowledge that our soul depends on to survive. As our reality improves, our minds unleash the proper Knowledge. We can draw to Earth much-needed support from other planets. We are finally becoming enlightened in our reality and opening our -minds as we elevate to new levels of understanding. We are creating reality that attaches to our spirit. We are connecting to all dimensions of all loving realities of the universe.

What is the Higher Realm? How does it connect to our higher self, here in this reality? Each of us have a higher part of who we are, being in another dimension of reality. For instance, when things occur in this consciousness of life, they create a certain mental reaction. Emotions of hatred, jealousy, fear, limitation, sadness, or revenge might appear and pour from us. This unconscious action unwittingly prevents the reality of our higher selves to surface.

The energy of our being survives physical death. Only that energy can ascend to the anointed one. As we understand our reality more fully, the powers of both realms will become one. We cannot achieve this while we live and breathe. In this state we are limited and controlled.

We can connect to the other civilizations of the Cosmos through the vortex in our minds, which has no limits of space or time. Once we acknowledge it as true and real, we can begin to understand it as the method responsible for our ability to astral project and visit these other realms.

There are two worlds connected by one reality to this Earth; the reality of truth and light of our higher selves, and the reality of darkness and fear. One is the origins of our feminine energy of light, while the other is the corrupted form of alien, masculine energy, used to instill fear and enslave others. The corrupted male energy in our existence is obvious. Feminine energy can also be corrupted, as evidenced by one's desire to control or to dominate. The energy harboring traits of either gender can be disguised in the opposite physical body.

We must remain vigilant and cognizant that controlling influences constantly seek to shackle our minds, desires, behaviors, our lives.Free Will is always within your grasp to use your own mind to reach the highest realm of all realities. The world must make the critical decision to unite and walk this path together. We must listen for the inner voice of Christ to guide our lives.

His life was sacrificed so we could be given an opportunity to be free from the tyrants in this consciousness. He opposes the enslavement of the mind. He wants every spirit to understand their power of Free Will. It makes no difference of your choice of religion or your ethnicity. He simply wants us all to increase the knowledge of his purpose and agenda.

He ascended with Knowledge of pure love and forgiveness toward the ones who placed the false reality of taxes and commerce ahead of his purpose over two thousand years ago. From the exact moment he asked the higher realm to "forgive them, for they knew not what they had done," he ascended with the power of love. It was to assist us in our accomplishments, to help us to prevail against an illusory reality within our mind and world. Christ's purpose has everything to do with our success in freeing our own spirit from this doomed reality.

The "Anointed One" has chosen certain ones to work in this realm on behalf of the Higher Realm. There is progress around the world occurring daily. Coming to our world is the collapse of this alien system, and the opportunity of self-improvement for each human to experience the purpose of Christ and why he came to save us all. For him to once again return to Earth, we must change. Our dark reality has kept him away. We must be mentally strong in the correct reality before he will return.

# REVEALED KNOWLEDGE

▲ The unique Source of our Knowledge exists in our Universe and can be seen from anywhere on Planet Earth, what we refer to as home.

▲ Earth has become a constant residual of our Alchemy of existence that has been altered and reformed through programming of the mind for what seems like centuries.

▲ There are many clues that lead to Orion as our celestial home. We must raise our own consciousness while we are here to remain permanently in Orion's three cycles of consciousness.

▲ Christ and his reality of love reigns over our consciousness – the consciousness man has been ruling by lies and manipulation in order enslave all beings and force them to be reborn to serve their own selfish purposes.

▲ The two realms in which energies are dominating are Earth and our celestial home in Orion.

▲ The energy of Orion is Feminine Love, the same energy that once mirrored our consciousness here on Earth, before it shifted to become man's rule, controlled by conflict, murder, and other acts of violence.

▲ Of the two realms, only one has great power. In the realm hijacked by man, energy can live in the opposite vessel of gender. This explains the existence of soft male genders that are not necessarily gay. However, homosexuality is a sign of the opposite energy in the opposite gender. This is a power tool of the Higher Realm. It is important for balance that each gender is experienced by the energy, to avoid being drawn to war.

▲ In the Higher Realm, there are no hidden disguises; the soul is of either of male energy or feminine energy. In this reality, however, the soul can reside in the opposite gender of anatomy. I can speak for myself and countless others who are female now, but surely know they were a male in their original form. While I possess great Knowledge, I also love as feminine energy loves.

# NOTES

# NOTES

# 14

## MY WALK WITH CHRIST

What exactly did Christ mean when he spoke the words, "You will have eternal life?" I believe that he was describing the Knowledge of your soul and its energy (the spirit). It is a fact of universal science. Your soul cannot be destroyed, ever. For the soul's spirit to be known, it must exist in a vessel, a body, made up of Earthly elements. The soul's spirit gives that vessel life!

Now that we have this better understanding of ourselves, it is time for the ultimate truth. That truth is that we are to live in many dimensions of reality within three cycles and three Perils. What Christ meant for us to understand is that he will be with us through the end of the Ages, and that throughout these Ages, all spirits will exist in many bodies in either gender.

We must recognize that recalling our previous lives is not our normal behavior. To accomplish it we must plant the seed of thought and with time and nurturing, it will become the intention of the spirit who manifested it. I have done so in my life. I understand that I have lived many lives over an extensive amount of time. During each lifespan, I expired before mastering the Knowledge. This was due to the actions of others in these past lifetimes. They successfully destroyed my vessel, forcing my spirit out of this reality and consciousness, time after time after time. Finally, during this lifetime, my achievement is fulfilled, at long, long last!

I can remember vividly a guide I encountered during an astral momentous journey. He appeared as a medium-height man. He spoke to me, relating the importance of returning with the blessing and power of the "Anointed One", provided that my Free Will cooperated without influence. It had to be my voluntary decision and every detail mattered to this reality.

He made clear why I would be this special messenger to Earth. He said that the Knowledge must be presented by a being that had experienced suffering on many levels. Unfortunately, I met that qualification, yet my heart remained fully open and forgiving. I knew that our greatest human attribute is the power to forgive. I understood that all humankind needed to acquire this reality of Knowledge while in this consciousness, allowing the spirit to experience a reality that is not influenced by the system of man.

It was all so much to ingest at once...my being called by the Higher Realm to help bring people to a place that I barely understood myself. I had so much to learn about my purpose. It was difficult not to feel unworthy of it all. I knew I had to learn what the "Anointed One" had instructed me to execute and complete. I was to seek the mirrored Knowledge of my soul. Once I discovered it, I would teach the Alchemy of the soul, spirit, and mind, along with Love and Gratitude.

This was the essence of the message of the pyramid. Its existence represents the reality from the Highest Realm. It is a symbol of our celestial home, within the planets of Orion. It is a sacred symbol of a dimension that our spirits, when fully prepared, will return to join with our soul completely as one.

I realized Christ was right: not only must I overcome my own fear and ignorance, but also relearn this Knowledge and purpose. I also promised to help as many people as possible before the Third Peril debuts, which is now upon us. Christ told me I'd have help and guidance and He kept his word. Through astral travels during my sleeping hours, I have met many others who assisted me in his plan to save as many spirits as possible. The evidence of this movement is overwhelming and urgent.

For three days I was in the Higher Realm, witnessing, experiencing, learning, and being instructed. On the third day I was required to return to our dark, dense, reality. When I awoke in the hospital from my coma, I had no memory of any of the events I just described. Instead, I had an overwhelming desire to live and survive. Today, I understand why I could not remember. It was because the cells in my body mirrored this reality, creating a super dense shield for thoughts, separating me from the real experience of the "Anointed One" and the Higher Realm. Also hidden, waiting to be unlocked was my encrypted Knowledge.

Time passed. For the following three years, I lived the life I had previously led, unaware of the revelations I experienced months earlier during my 72-hour coma. Then it began. I can best describe it as an energy, invisible, seeming to shadow my every move. I was sensing that I was about to recall something important, as though it was on the tip of my tongue. Unfortunately, I remained in a daze, ignorant of any meaning. Over time, the anxiety surrounding this feeling became more intense. I began to question my sanity. I was more and more heading toward something...but what?

The memories of my revelation of being physically before Jesus Christ, the "Anointed One", began to return, slowly pressing into my spirit and mind, demanding that I seek my purpose. It finally became clear as a full recall happened. I had been returned to the living so that I could attempt what I had failed to do before. In this current cycle, I would master the Knowledge. I was to write the truth of our power and our purpose.

Now, no matter what I face in the future, I am mentally and physically prepared for what awaits me. Because I returned here voluntarily, with the wisdom of Christ and his true intention, I can live out my word to honor and respect his purpose. I had to look deeply into who I was and walk away from the luxurious life to which I had long grown accustomed. I had to fix my gaze outward as well, staring into the unknown, with trust and love as my guides

Had I resisted and ignored the signs that led me to self-discovery, I would not have advanced in my Knowledge and understanding. It is a blessing that I am stubborn. I refused to forsake the opportunity to savor freedom, the most precious gift of life. I am happy for the world. I know this book will serve a great purpose. It will forever remind us of our origins and the Christ Consciousness we have allowed to be hidden from our minds.

## REVEALED KNOWLEDGE

▲ Any progress made was reversed by acts of man, yet Christ remains a part of our lives through each cycle, collectively raising the bar to raise the consciousness.

▲ What does eternal life mean? It means you will live for eternity; the question is, which reality will that be, the one man has hijacked in the present reality or in Orion? What we learn here in the powerful consciousness we exist in determines that outcome.

▲ The Knowledge of Christ was to provide the path back to him and the feminine realm. We return to each cycle with the intention to master his Knowledge that is encrypted in our DNA. It lies dormant in all of us.

▲ Our greatest purpose is to raise our reality to save the consciousness of this eternal energy. We can choose to exist, or we can increase our vibration and look deeper into ourselves. The tool is our discovery of the reality of eternal life; the more we can understand and grasp, the better. The meaning of eternal life speaks volumes. We have lived many lives before the current one. But because our spirit has been smothered with the events of man in each life, we cannot recall them.

▲ Engaging in war is an eternal practice while we are under man's spell. Such violent events embed themselves into our cells and force each being to reincarnate to re-experience what he or she has already experienced in multiple past lives: endless war in a habitual cycle. These are signs we fail to recognize in the current life. Many will be encouraged to enlist by their parents or promises from their government.

▲ There must be a greater purpose to life than killing other spirits whose minds have been manipulated and taught only fear and ignorance. These spirits reincarnate to live in the same conditions, with no hope of raising their consciousness, due to the limited amount of resources they have.

# NOTES

# NOTES

# 15

# THE KNOWLEDGE THAT MUST BE LEARNED IN THE CURRENT CONSCIOUSNESS

Two important facts must be fully and completely understood: first, there is no death, and second, the Knowledge and purpose of the true state of consciousness must be mastered while in this dimension of reality, Whatever your level of formal academic education, your mastery of any worldly trades, crafts, or professions will not guarantee you passage to the Higher Realm. Your spirit will be redirected back, either to Earth or another life-sustaining planet where humans can learn lessons. We will reincarnate as many times as required while Earth is still spinning or until Free Will has successfully activated the encrypted code of the "Anointed One" and our purpose.

Only this coded "soul" Knowledge will free us from the enslavement of the invading darkness. We must release all worldly possessions to obtain our ticket to the Higher Realm. Love = Knowledge + Power. It belongs to the expanded mind that has reached complete freedom by embracing and understanding that we have had a choice the whole time through our own Free Will.

When I refer to worldly possessions, I mean our emotional attachments to material items. Releasing this attachment is key to experiencing the Highest Realm. Learning to give to others, instead of merely receiving, begins the process of finally allowing us to achieve true self-worth. Many seek material things as a means of coping and self-aggrandizement, with the false notion that it will result in healing. But the healing never comes. It is a truth we must accept.

Material things should flow from our desires to express love, both for oneself and for others. It should never be a replacement for the true emotion of love. When one gives from the heart, the action proves that love has overcome fear and self-limitation. The mind has become (or is becoming) enlightened. We must release all attachment to anything or anyone in this realm. Only your spirit can return to its soul.

We must un-learn many of the tenets of our dark reality that we have been taught to believe. Contrary to the false teachings, we are not weak and powerless. We do not exist to crave material possessions. The negative dogma instills fear and perpetuates the myth that we should sacrifice our eternal spirits for the selfish whims of the few. It is folly to lavish love on material possessions that are spiritless and inert.

Once upon a time, it was a practice to give all your worldly possessions away, then to replenish the supply by using the Knowledge to create more. That existence will have a renaissance. When the mind can grasp the methods of how all things are created, it becomes evident that anyone can do this. What prevents a spirit from graduating to this level is the imprinted, accepted, or implied suggestions of another individual or a group. We will take back our power by expanding our minds and experiencing creation by thought. Our thoughts must imprint our future.

An example of imprinting is prayer. When you pray for another person, believing you are helping them and trusting that what you pray for will come to pass, you are imprinting goodwill to that person at his or her time of need. When the mind is unsure and limited, anything that is presented will most likely be accepted and become the reality. This explains why many people receive mixed results, claiming that prayers are not answered. This is also how people place themselves in high financial debts, believing it is the way to achieve what their desires. Man's way of obtaining material experiences is through the practice of a method that supports their system.

Expanding the mind to connect to dimensions beyond this current reality is how a spirit can create and experience in ways only conjured in dreams.

We should act as role models for those around us who have never known how to use their minds in a way that would achieve all they could imagine. Society often refers to such people as "less fortunate." We must help each other and give Love and Gratitude to the world, by practicing these powerful laws, or we will continue to waste precious time.

Many believe that what they deal with daily is real.

For instance, consider the laws that we live under in this dark reality. Think of how our court systems operate. Laws are supposed to stand for "justice for all," but the truth is far different. The reality of inequity is what the system we exist under practices daily. This perpetuates their purpose.

While we may be unaware of the controls that bind us, we are surely lashed to this reality. Currency is a concept that was created to control society, by forcing us to labor. We earn currency so that we may live in an Earthly society. We are taught that we have no real ownership of our energy, and that we are forever obliged to be dependent upon the few who control this planet through multiple programmed realities.

Work and labor are not the cause of our misery. Instead, it is the currency and how it is used to control. We must understand that currency alone has no power or value, until assigned a specific value by the controllers.

To escape the illusion that everything in our lives of valuable is measurable in a currency we must do several things. We must acknowledge our environment by recognizing what is going on in our home or workplace. Also, we must know who our business associates are, in truth. Do these things and we will change the family, work, and power dynamics to reflect what it is intended to be for our lives.

The illusion of monetary wealth was created as a program for our minds. Its purpose was to prove to us that wealth and status are most important. However, in the Higher Realm, such people are regarded as simply foolish. In the final analysis, who gains from this reality? I believe it is the spiritual seekers. They are unattached to physical wealth (but can create what they need at any time). They abide by Universal Laws.

Neither man nor woman will reach the highest realm in this consciousness by placing desire in the material realm. Love is the highest vibration to know and experience. It will fill the holes in your heart. You will be complete from within. The science of this Knowledge will show you that love for the world is far more important to than anything you have or will ever have. You will feel amazed and excited in anticipation of the moment of its arrival.

Just know that your desires are not self-directed, but for all to see and experience. Feel as if you have reconnected to your past and the Knowledge you once had, which has been a part of you, even without your knowing. This Knowledge will release the burden of not feeling loved, because now you can focus on other people and give all the love inside of you to those who reside in the consciousness with you. The reality of Christ's Knowledge has been among us since he walked the hills of Galilee. His return depends on our being mentally prepared. Please understand that fact. We must be a mirror of his love.

# REVEALED KNOWLEDGE

▲ To elevate the mind's ability to discover a grander purpose besides the intruders system we must obtain the true Knowledge.

▲ History reveals the government and the people, and the ones who rebelled against the rule of government.

▲ With Knowledge of history removed from the minds of future generations, they will inherit total domination of all governments. Their rights will be limited.

▲ The next agenda will be to remove all religions: Judaism and the Jewish Torah, Christianity and Christianity's Bible, and Islam and the Muslim Koran.

▲ With history and religions eviscerated, it will erase the one entity from the existence of future generations: The Anointed One, Christ.

▲ The Higher Realm has been dismantling the alien force within the Government for quite some time. Don't fret about history and religion; remember, both were part of the schemes of prior times. Created by an invading force, carried out by our own brother and sisters who lost their way, as a result many have suffered throughout history.

▲ The Anointed One promised he would not ever abandon us and would be with us through the ages. The time has come for him to return, but certain things that must be done prior to his arrival.

▲ We must improve our reality by saving our consciousness together. It is not enough to have only a few million awaken. His mind needs to connect to our minds. It starts with the four-letter word, LOVE. The Anointed One, Christ, needs us to forgive all others and their trespasses. He needs us to LOVE each other unconditionally and stop judging. Lack of knowing causes mistakes. In this case, the mistake is in forgetting that our higher powers that are still within us all.

▲ If any religion works, why is the world so lost and confused? The answer is it doesn't work; it is all part of a grander scheme to control, manipulate, and enslave the mind and reality.

# NOTES

# 16

## THE KNOWLEDGE REQUIRED IN THE HIGHER REALM

The "Anointed One" is our connection to the blueprint of the Higher Realm. Only the Knowledge of superior wealth, which is Love, will be admitted and accepted in the Higher Realm, though the tangible matter that has been created will continue to exist here on Earth. I discovered that, in our remote past, we could recall our previous lives.. We were required to return here, to continue to expand our minds to the highest achievement of Knowledge. Then, we would advance to the next appropriate dimension of reality, depending upon our previously achieved Knowledge. I know there is no end to life or to the Knowledge of our source energy.

We reincarnate because the incorrect knowledge we practiced and created by the dark design of the alien invaders and their issue inhibits our natural ability to use our minds to expand. That is why we fail. The Knowledge in this book was suppressed and buried away because the programming from the occupiers created a false reality, layered into our energy bodies, attaching to our cells. I believe, with every fiber of my being, that once our minds have been restored to their original Knowledge of the Laws of our source creator, we will remember what we created in a previous life, and we will pick up where our Knowledge left off, at the beginning of the Bronze Age, before the invading alien race's system imposed the Iron Age of darkness on our reality.

Upon our cycle's end, we must not leave behind any attachment to any material possession or item. We require 100% of our energy. If we fail, the material item absorbs much of our energy within our reality and the spirit delivers limitation in all areas to the Higher Realm of reality. The pharaohs who attempted to carry the energy of their possessions back with their spirits, believing it was a great offering of their accomplishments, were confused by their Knowledge of being able to travel through matter. Yet they also knew that only the energy of the objects, not the objects themselves, could be carried back with them to the other realm upon their cycle ending. They did not realize that the spirit recorded everything in the cells, both good and bad. There was no need to show their attachment to objects by being buried with them. Sadly, it only demonstrated their limitation to the Higher Realm.

The science was mastered very well by the Egyptians, but its purpose was to create and remain strong, not to become attached to this realm. The Egyptians believed that we must hold material to be wealthy. It was a mistake made by the Pharaohs. All matter, and its energy, must remain here in this plane. Our energy must return to its natural plane in the Cosmos of Orion, unattached to the elements of Earth. We are to ascend with our collective achievements while we are here. The lack of awareness and understanding of this Knowledge will indefinitely hold us to this realm if we fail to relinquish attachment to physical matter.

When we ascend to the Higher Realm, it will only be temporary, unless the superior Laws of the Universe have been mastered and fully understood. The spirit must be decoded completely from practicing the invading aliens' programs, and the layers of their programming must be removed prior to the ending of the cycle, so that the current layer of reality can completely be eviscerated while we still exist in this most powerful state of being in the current consciousness.

To know Love and Gratitude is to know the "Anointed One's" Knowledge. It is to exist in a reality of equality for all, where there is no limitation or need for anything except love. Once the mind has mastered Alchemy and the understanding of the science that creates all things, it will be known that one can create, then give it all away, and then recreate the very same and even more. If we are granted the gift of Knowledge which could help another, but fail to share it with them, it is a sign of our weakness and ignorance; it also signals that we exist in a reality of limitation from within. This action or choice of the personality prevents the spirit from finding its true potential and freedom.

The Third Peril is fast approaching, and it cannot be stopped. Earth is in the final stages of warning, as the expansion has already begun. The crust will eventually separate, as it has in the remote past, allowing poisonous gases to encompass our atmosphere, eliminating human life. Other life forms will be affected and cease to exist. The Third Peril will compromise this planet and its ability to sustain life, whether by self-destruction, war by our own hands, or some other event. This event is fastly approaching us. When the time arrives,where will the energy of the souls go to learn? Once the Earth can no longer sustain life in the flesh and mass depopulation takes place, spirits cannot return anymore and become trapped in a dimension. The rapture will be the higher dimensions orchestrating a third time rescue for many enlightened humans by the United Alien Force of light– the United Federation of Light of Other Galaxies -- which has been patiently awaiting our enlightenment. Their aim is to aid us in preventing the rediscovered Knowledge from being lost by such an event while in this powerful consciousness. All life organisms will endure this event, not just culpable humans. I fully realize and remember the destruction Earth is capable of inflicting on all organisms of life from experiencing the end of the previous Age. She knows when too much resources have been utilized and must reclaim them to expand and comply with the ever expanding Universe she is following.

Unless we expand our minds and open our hearts, a buffer zone of darkness will no doubt become our permanent destination for eternity or until we can correct our DNA. If that happens, the energy (spirit) of many will be lost, because Earth was created so that we could evolve and move to higher dimensions of reality. Instead, we repeat the same habits because of our programming, which can be corrected with proper thinking and practice, instead of delusional thinking. Those who believe themselves worthy of existing in the Higher Realm despite their self-centered baggage; selfish and greedy mindset, or fear-and-hate-filled hearts are so deluded.

The kingdom of Christ (heaven), is a real place in the Cosmos. If the mind does not learn this Knowledge as quickly as possible while in the conscious state, the spirit is lost from ever returning to its soul that is waiting to be whole again. The remaining chances to learn are diminishing, and the opportunities we have been given will run out upon 2033 the planet we have been residing on no longer exists to sustain life in the flesh. We must no longer exist in a reality of fear or limitation

The Alien force created the HAARP program. It exists to prevent a rescue of humans by other beings from the light. HAARP is a system designed by both private and government entities. It consists of an adjustable microwave signal, a very low, vibratory signal sent to a desired location on the surface of the Earth, by bouncing it off the ionosphere, or sending it into space, where it is shaped around the planet by satellites. The 12 vortices that align the Earth were created by each expansion of this planet, creating a rip in her atmosphere allowing spaceships, visiting from other galaxies, to travel by means of the magnetic pull that these vortices create. These vortices are referred to as the Bermuda Triangle and similar areas, benefiting the purpose of the HAARP program.

There are numerous HAARP plants on all continents. They create a complete shield of microwave signals around the planet, heating our atmosphere and spreading throughout different countries. Each grid consists of seventy towers, approximately 170 feet in height. Their purpose is to counter and disrupt the vortices that are affecting the natural process of Earth, and our normal patterns of thought.

The result? Discontinuity of thought for us. These towers also have step-down transformers in every neighborhood for future manipulation of our thoughts. The frequencies for causing these reactions in our brains were researched decades ago. I felt a surge to my brain one evening passing by a power grid along a highway.

Each HAARP grid operates with approximately one million watts. It has bases around planet Earth, in the form of a grid that sends dangerously powerful, high-frequency beams into space, creating a shield around the planet. This technology is designed so that nothing can come into or go out of our atmosphere, and if any object does, it will end up like the Discovery space shuttle that disintegrated over the state of Texas when it entered Earth's atmosphere back in the early nineties. What we are facing is the microwave HAARP that will only cause havoc here on the ground and affect the minds of all humans and animals. The time has come to start using our minds productively for a better cause for the entire planet. Consider the idea of Earth being unable to sustain the proper atmosphere required for our survival. In a previous chapter it was noted the intention of colonizing Mars. The entire Universe is expanding constantly and impacts all matter within the sphere.

We were not created by man but were programmed to exist under laws that interrupt and disrupt our purpose here: to expand our minds with superior Knowledge and to express the emotion of love to each other. Without these two realities of our source creator, we return in our next lives with the limitation of knowledge that is strictly designed to work for the benefit of those in charge of commerce, which again supports the reality and environment designed by an invading alien force. If a spirit ascends with a mind that has not been purified from this reality, that soul's spirit will be prevented from remaining in the Higher Reality.

# REVEALED KNOWLEDGE

- ▲ Love, Forgiveness and Non-judgement are the three most important codes to live by.
- ▲ Love, Forgiveness and Non-judgement share a unique bond for our purpose: they help us all to ascend to greater heights of existence. It feels quite empowering when a violation occurs, isn't taken personally, and is forgiven automatically. This can range from minor to severe acts. The point is an open heart does not allow feelings of revenge. Remember, we all are here temporarily. We will cross over for different reasons, good and bad. Keep in mind that things are done deliberately to incite the emotions of fear, hatred, and revenge.
- ▲ No matter how a life cycle ends, there is still no reality of death – just a transition of energy from an enslavement to a beautiful reality of pure, unconditional love. Imagine what our world would be like without hatred and wicked teachings to believe in phantom gods that truly originated from Egyptian doctrines.
- ▲ The Higher Realm is made up of great Knowledge and unconditional Love. In this most beautiful realm, great spirits are also referred to as angels who watch over us.
- ▲ The obsession to survive in this man-created system began in many previous lives. It has been instilled and driven into the depths of our cells. In each new life cycle, we are more than willing to cooperate with the system's design. Often, people try to resist, but eventually give in and become contributors. Many sanctions are threatened against anyone who revolts against man's diabolical practices to maintain his claim ownership over the entire world.
- ▲ There is one way to put an end to their madness, which does not require violence: the power of the mind. Only through concentrated focus on the experience of love can the thinking mind improve this reality in an instant. I am not talking about a romantic love, with its requirement

of personal intimacy. That alone holds all the power and confuses unconditional love.

▲ Why would the United States government bring to the US soil a culture that completely lives in a totally different realm of reality, due to its own government? Because they have been planning this one world takeover for at least half a century.

▲ This Knowledge is not just mine, it belongs to everyone! The Higher Realm is no longer turning a blind eye when spirits cross over. That pitiful excuse "I did not know," is no longer is accepted, and I am glad. Some of us are tired of reincarnating to repeat the same warnings, only to have people ignore them and refuse to wake up. It isn't fair for anyone to be committed to a purpose when miniscule progress has been made. Many of us have suffered due to the lack and ignorance of others.

▲ A cycle is for a specific amount of time, so what sense does it make to accumulate more than you really need? It is totally dangerous, mentally obsessive, and unhealthy. It's also a sign that the person hasn't a clue about what comes before and after a life cycle.

# NOTES

# NOTES

# 17

# THE PATH WE MUST CHOOSE TO WALK

The most important themes presented throughout this book, are the approaching Third Peril, changing our consciousness, and understanding the magnitude of what we are all facing in the future. We must be prepared for the aftermath of the expansion of Earth and what it will mean to us all, both physically and emotionally. But, more importantly, we must do everything in our power to disallow the same usurpers to continue the mental control they have exercised on us all since the days of Exodus.

At this moment, we can become again the powerful beings we once were. The destruction of this planet will yield a multitude of effects from homelessness, loss of technology, and massive loss of life. This is part of the contract of being here in a physical form. The usurpers are fully aware of the oncoming Peril, and they are fully prepared to do what is necessary to continue to rule the reality and enslave our minds.

To save our consciousness, we all must stand together as one body of people. All cultures will then be in a sacred reality of love and light. Saving our physical existence in this life cycle is not a realistic goal. However, if we improve our energy of thought and how we exist, we will save our consciousness for future life.

For thousands of years we have had "The Eight Ball, Their Reality" blocking us from connecting back to our higher selves. By not improving our mental capacity right now, guarantees continued repression. We have so much to do, and we are doing it! No longer acknowledging their control as real. I realize the obsession with material wealth. It isn't easy to relinquish objects that represents achievement of your life. Everyone will need to make a critical choice to determine what is most important. Physical wealth or

Mental wealth? This book is intended for everyone! My focus is on the meek by personal choice. The "Anointed One" focuses on all people both wealthy and limited to improve and exist in a mind and heart of knowledge and love.

The fear is no longer within our minds, the fear is now in their minds of the oppressors! They realize the awakening at hand. They fear losing their reality of control in which they have used our knowledge to enslave us. We have prevailed against their practices. Now is the time to listen, learn and share! Talk to each other, stop doubting freedom from their reality. The doubt is their programming of the mind. Doubting creates fear, fear shuts down the mind. Regardless of when your life cycle ends, what you have in your heart and in your mind is the purpose here.

We must not comply with their agenda and reality. The planet is owned by none, but the reality was behind the Eight Ball, but not any longer. We all are brilliant! Knowledge has been limited and only provided to certain parts of the planet. This is how the system worked for the rulers who enjoyed the outcome of their false control. This information must be provided to all people! If a person can't read, then it needs to be taught or explained. We are not exempting anyone for any reason. People who have committed horrible acts must also be given this information. We are not here to judge, hate or discriminate against anyone. We are here to make a stand and commit to work hard mentally to improve our reality and love and help each other. Not any person can do this alone! We must unite on all levels and build each other up. We stand to lose a great deal if we fail. It is far better to die for a grand purpose than to be a frightened coward continuing to serve the invaders of this once peaceful planet. I pray that this message is taken very seriously! Only you, and all people, will benefit from grasping the importance of the road that stretches ahead.

# REVEALED KNOWLEDGE

▲ I cannot stress enough the urgency to make a quick discovery of the awakening before another destruction of Earth occurs. It is going to happen. Look at the planet from the past. We were one continent before it separated and created other countries.

▲ Just as a pregnant woman's womb expands to allow the infant to grow within her, Earth continues to expand along with her Universe. Man attempts to play god by constantly creating situations; from war, to the poisoning of both food and water, and the spraying of chemicals from aircraft to affect all organs of animals and humans.

▲ This fact is warning enough to raise your consciousness while you can. Earth has swallowed up evidence of the past progresses and we think this is all brand new to us. It is not. All we have and created was blue-printed into the cells of the one who created that invention. There is only one act to do, and that is to raise our consciousness. If society doesn't, it can be easily determined that both Earth and man will see you later. Why chance it or risk it? Raising the consciousness is all about the mind and changing paradigms. It will not cost anything that most believe matters. It is a consciousness move and a choice to think and separate man's system from what is real.

▲ Earth must expand to accommodate every life form, not just humans. She loves vegetation, animals and humans. Every species of life falls victim to her expansion. It is nothing personal, it is her being a mother and doing what is necessary to care for her visitors that overstay their welcome as parasites do. She must make new elements to replace what is taken from her. Raising the consciousness is the only way to freedom. Being here trapped would seem scarier to me then taking that first step to save oneself. It is a choice each person must face. I have done my best to convey how to do it and why it must be done.

▲ If you don't know how to start on the path, reach out to spiritual groups. These are groups that do not follow religion, although they may accept Christ as the savior, or at a minimum, exercise his wisdom. That is the most important thing to Christ: following his common sense. Love, forgive, and don't judge. Help others while helping yourself. If you can't help others, work on you and once you strengthen your own mind, you can share your experiences to enlighten those around you. This is a movement that requires us to collectively support each other while we are going through this major transition.

\A warm thank you, dear reader, for allowing my Knowledge to come your way through this book. Since the experience that changed my life forever, I have sought to be a true and clear messenger, nothing more or less. My life's mission is to share my insights without judgement or bias. You must, as an individual spirit, choose your own path forward. I seek only to illuminate your steps and encourage your journey.

Take my words as a truthful representation of what I know and believe for us all. I am just like you in so many ways. But unlike you, I have "seen such wonders", and been in the physical presence of Eternal Love and Goodness. Open your mind and dare to see your place in the vast Universe.

It is there, waiting for you to throw open the door and realize your true being. You are part of the whole. You are undying energy. You are everlasting.

# ACKNOWLEDGMENTS

All my Love and Gratitude is to Christ, for guiding me and imparting to me his superior Knowledge, including the meaning of Love and Gratitude. I am grateful to John the Baptist for speaking up and telling me I did not have to step down from this purpose and mission, if I chose not to. Overall, my awareness of Love and Gratitude are of Christ, and Christ sustains my Free Will to have power in both realities. I want to thank and give praise to all the people whom Christ, his disciples, and the three angels handpicked for me to meet on my path in this life, who have prepared me for my journey home.

I would like to express Love and Gratitude to my daughter, Crista M. I would also like to express Love and Gratitude to my Chief Editor Engineer of communication, Chuck Gillespie. His ability to articulate this knowledge and bring my discoveries to life has been an astounding experience! Gratitude to all the proofreaders, Crista McLeod, Daria Anne DiGiovanni, Terra Jarvis, Jennifer Carless.

I harbor within me,Love and Gratitude to my late parents. My loving mother, Mrs. Joann Grauberger, who will always be a beautiful woman, in her loving spirit. She is greatly missed, but I will see her again. To my beloved father, Mr. Wade W. Pearce. Thank you for namingme Melinda, a name with such a profound meaning( Black and Beautiful). In this current cycle of life, I have amassed great Knowledge. I'm thrilled to share it with the entire planet.

A specific event, I will always remember ,my father contacting me after he passed to the other side. Speaking to me through my mind, to tell me how proud he was of me, and how much he loved me. It meant everything, to hear his voice in my mind for the first time ever, assuring me he loved me during this life. It's an experience I will retain in my cells in this cycle of existence. My father saw my future and my purpose. He was proud of me, knowing what I was about to do for both realities.

My greatest Love and Gratitude goes to all my children and grandchildren. I pray they all will seek the correct way of existing, and not continue to remain trapped in this false reality of the culprits who misuse the purpose for being here. (in order of age): Crista, my firstborn, you have always had a heart of pure gold. I love you, Daughter. My son, Darrel – when I see you, I know that within your spirit is Christ-intention. A fine Law Enforcement Officer. You are a wonderful father to your daughter, my granddaughter, Arianna. I love you, Son. I give an abundance of Love and Gratitude to my middle child, Michelle. You are very strong-minded, and you love helping others in any way you possibly can. You are a go-getter and doer. You are a fantastic mother to your daughter, Samantha Asha, my firstborn grandchild, and to your son, my grandson, Jack (RJ) a beautiful wife to your husband Jonathan. I love you, Daughter. I send Love and Gratitude to my daughter, Tiffany, who has a creative side about her. Your sons and daughters, my grandchildren, Robert, Brandon, Cheyenne and Kharlee Renae Smith. I love you, Daughter. My son Charles, you have always been the one who could reason and follow by thinking; though you may not understand it all, you certainly understand the science. I love you Charlie boy, aka Chuck.

To the Bohemian people of Nassau Bahamas: during my recent visit to Atlantis, I discovered the knowledge you harbor in your cells. As we spoke, the spirit of Knowledge in you surfaced, assuring me, we both knew the truth. My connection to you exists through my past lives. Our paths were meant to cross once again to validate our knowledge. My extended family participated in building Atlantis. My Uncle Clarence L. Pearce assisted in the development of forming the massive concrete pours of the resort's foundations. I am forever grateful for the gentleman from South Africa named Saul Kirshner, who designed Atlantis to be a reality of the culture who taught us great Knowledge in the very beginning, namely the Africans from bygone ages. The real civilization of Atlantis still exists today as part of a perfect reality. Many believe Atlantis to be a myth and has been long forgotten. But, I can assure all, it is still in existence. I know, I have visited that realm twice now. It is underwater in a huge dome. The purpose is connected to the three suns of Orion and our minds.

Sincerely,
Melynda Pearce

www.ingramcontent.com/pod-product-compliance
Lightning Source LLC
Chambersburg PA
CBHW072127090426

42739CB00012B/3102